Meredith Nicholson
A Writing Life

INDIANA BIOGRAPHY SERIES

Meredith Nicholson

A Writing Life

RALPH D. GRAY

GENERAL EDITORS

RAY E. BOOMHOWER AND RACHEL M. POPMA

INDIANA HISTORICAL SOCIETY PRESS

INDIANAPOLIS 2007

© 2007 Indiana Historical Society Press. All rights reserved.
This book is a publication of the
Indiana Historical Society Press
450 West Ohio Street
Indianapolis, Indiana 46202-3269 USA
www.indianahistory.org
Telephone orders 1-800-447-1830
Fax orders 317-234-0562
Order online @ http://shop.indianahistory.org

Library of Congress Cataloging-in-Publication Data

Gray, Ralph D.
    Meredith Nicholson : a writing life / Ralph D. Gray.
        p. cm. — (Indiana biography series)
    Includes bibliographical references.
    ISBN 978-0-87195-257-8 (cloth : alk. paper)
        1. Nicholson, Meredith, 1866–1947. 2. Authors, American—20th
    century—Biography. 3. Indiana—Intellectual life. I. Title.

    PS3527.I35Z67 2007
    977.2—dc22
    [B]

                                                2007012737

Printed in Canada

*This book is dedicated to the Van Vorst
and Gray siblings, Jim, Chuck, and Charlie,
and to the memory of John and Robert,
real Hoosiers all, no matter where they lived,
and to all others who, like Meredith Nicholson,
love Indiana.*

". . . the real man is in his books."
Professor George E. Woodberry

TABLE OF CONTENTS

Stand Up for Indiana

*"The strong arm of the Hoosier commonwealth
will be thrown protectingly around every Indiana
soldier in this war, as in wars of the past. Stand up
and be counted for Indiana."*[1]

MEREDITH NICHOLSON, 1917

AS HIS BIBLIOGRAPHERS HAVE NOTED, MEREDITH NICHOLSON loved Indiana, and as their bibliography demonstrated, he loved to write, especially about his native state. The title of a newspaper article he wrote in July 1917, used here as the title for this introduction, seems appropriate, not only as a metaphor for Nicholson's entire writing life but as an example of his patriotism in times of trouble, in this case the "Great War," 1914–18, which the United States entered in 1917.[2]

The foreword that Nicholson contributed to *A Book of Indiana* (1929), compiled by his close friend and fellow newspaperman Frank McKinney "Kin" Hubbard (famed as the creator of the rustic Abe Martin from Brown County), contains perhaps Nicholson's most extreme statement of his state pride. In a delightful spoof, praising the state beyond belief, Nicholson began by saying "the purpose of this Indiana handbook and gazetteer is to make residents of other states dissatisfied with their homes and bring them in haste to the grand old Hoosier commonwealth. It is inconceivable

Meredith Nicholson.

that any one fully advised as to Indiana's greatness would live elsewhere unless forcibly restrained by legal process." He conceded that the "original Garden of Eden" was probably elsewhere, but asserted that Indiana was a "land of opportunity, with advantages and privileges enjoyed by no other state, principality, kingdom or power." Having concluded that it would be impossible "to enumerate the infinite variety of products that have carried her fame into every port of the seven seas," he decided it would be "much simpler to mention the few things Indiana does not produce." This list included cotton, indigo, bananas, rice, hashish, "the dromedary, camel, and ostrich," and various citrus fruits and saltwater creatures. "Otherwise," Nicholson asserted boldly, "Indiana has been highly favored by Nature, the genius of man and the protective tariff" to the extent that "everything that can be wrought of iron, wood, steel, tin, glass, paper, stone, sand, broom straw or ink is manufactured within the state's borders." Lastly, he could not resist giving a boost to Indiana's tomatoes and cantaloupes, "the most flavorsome produced in America," pointing out that these items were "the highest priced on New York bills-of-fare."[3]

Indiana literary historian Arthur W. Shumaker of DePauw University has called Nicholson the "most rabid" of Indiana's major authors. More so than George Ade and Booth Tarkington, both of whom wrote books and plays set in Indiana, Nicholson was an outspoken advocate of all things Hoosier, and he was quick to take affront at any oversight by other writers regarding his state. His *Atlantic Monthly* article titled "Indianapolis: A City of Homes" was a stout defense of the virtues of his adopted city, which some of his fellow novelists in the East occasionally confused with Minneapolis or placed on the "Way-bosh" River rather than the White.[4]

Nicholson's novels, too, were often set in Indianapolis or other locales in central Indiana, and he consistently portrayed a community of diligent citizens doing their best. Although his first novel, *The Main Chance* (1903), was set in Omaha, Nebraska (his wife's hometown), his second and third romances and many subsequent ones had Indiana settings. *Zelda Dameron* (1904), a popular account of a young woman's coming of age in the state's capital city, used the device of having the heroine return to the community after an extended absence abroad so that the author could explore and describe the city's very changed appearance to the "newcomer" (and to his readers) at the turn of the century. Its new streets, some of which in the downtown area were now paved; the new public buildings; and the city's social and cultural amenities all received attention from the author's fertile pen. Zelda herself was a most appealing young woman—one reviewer said any man with a daughter would want her to be exactly like Zelda Dameron—and the book itself gave strong indication that a new and talented novelist had arrived on the scene.

It was Nicholson's third and most successful novel, *The House of a Thousand Candles* (1905), however, that truly established him as a major Indiana novelist, one who proudly boasted of and boosted the Hoosier State. In fact, his motivation for the book was in part to demonstrate that a dashing, spine-tingling adventure/mystery need not be set in far-off exotic locales such as the then-popular Anthony Hope novel *The Prisoner of Zenda*, but that such romances could be set in his own beloved Indiana. His instincts proved to be correct, and *The House of a Thousand Candles*, which Nicholson often referred to as his "dripping tallows" book, became an immediate best seller, was translated and published in half a dozen languages and developed by others into a popular Broadway play, and served as the basis for two motion pictures of the same name. Over the years this book (back in print more than a century since its publication, the only Nicholson novel so honored) has sold more than a half-million copies.

But Nicholson, his critics, and latter-day readers all agree that his finest writing, and his most substantial and enduring contributions to American letters, can be found in his essays and articles. These heartfelt commentaries, of which there are hundreds, analyze American society of the early twentieth century in the heartland of America. Particularly of note are the essays collected in *The Valley of Democracy* (1918) and *The Man in the Street* (1921). Nicholson's enduring faith in "folks," the ordinary people of the Ohio and Mississippi valleys and the Midwest, his inherent belief in democracy and democratic values, and his unapologetic patriotism permeate his essays, some of which excoriated the Ku Klux Klan and upheld the rights and virtues of women, attitudes not always popular at the time.

These convictions, along a winning personality and inherent charm and vitality (plus nearly lifelong activity in the Democratic Party and the sudden onset of financial need in the early 1930s) led to Nicholson's final contributions to his country. In 1933 President Franklin

D. Roosevelt appointed this outstanding Hoosier novelist to be America's top diplomat in war-torn Paraguay. Nicholson served ably in this new environment and went on to serve in two other Latin American countries before retiring from public life in 1941.

My interest in Meredith Nicholson is a longstanding one. In 1979, while working on an Indiana history book, I was surprised to learn that Nicholson, alone of the so-called Big Four of the golden age of Indiana literature in the nineteenth century, had as yet no scholarly biography. Adequate studies of the others—James Whitcomb Riley, George Ade, and Booth Tarkington—exist, but there is nothing for Nicholson other than an invaluable bibliographic work on him and other writers from Crawfordville, Indiana, and a vast number of newspaper and magazine articles by and about the man. Nor is there a major collection of Nicholson's writings and correspondence in a library or private hands.

There are, however, scattered among major research libraries across the country an exceedingly large amount of correspondence and other writings, for he was a prolific letter writer too. Evidently Nicholson's frequent moves in the later stages of his life, the loss of his first wife and her careful file-gathering labors, and the carelessness of his second wife during their decadelong union, 1933–43, resulted in the loss and destruction of Nicholson's papers, so that what remains is a substantial, but scattered, num-

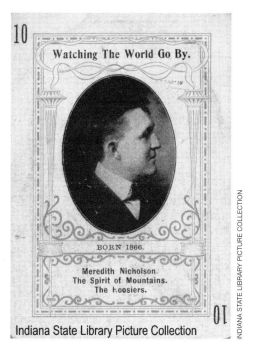

10

Watching The World Go By.

BORN 1866.

Meredith Nicholson.
The Spirit of Mountains.
The hoosiers.

Indiana State Library Picture Collection

INDIANA STATE LIBRARY PICTURE COLLECTION

*Nicholson is pictured in a set of Indiana
authors playing cards.*

ber of Nicholson letters among the collections and papers
of his friends and collaborators in libraries in North Carolina, Virginia, New Jersey, Massachusetts, and California,
as well as Indiana, especially in Indianapolis and Bloomington. A grandson and namesake, Meredith Nicholson
III, now living in Casa Grande, Arizona, has both a trunk
full of family papers and photographs and a large collection of the published writings of his famous relative. I am

grateful to "Med" for his kindness and generosity in sharing this material, along with family reminiscences, with me in recent years.

Another surprisingly rich cache of Nicholson writings is in the National Archives and Records Administration, which has among its vast holdings the monthly status reports and other documents that Nicholson filed throughout his eight-year tenure with the U.S. State Department. These dispatches sparkle with the author's wit, insight, and graceful style. Indeed, his counterparts in the diplomatic corps always looked forward to reading these epistles and lamented their disappearance when Nicholson was either transferred or, in 1941, permanently retired.

As indicated, I first became aware of the need for a Nicholson biography about twenty-five years ago, and said so in an Indiana "reader" I compiled at that time. Ironically, when I decided to look into filling that gap myself, I learned that Allegra Stewart, a professor at Butler University, had just undertaken such a study. She had been asked to do so by Nicholson's daughter-in-law, Roberta West Nicholson, who had herself been reminded of that bibliographic lapse in Indiana's history upon reading my book. Unfortunately, Stewart's interesting and quite helpful manuscript on Nicholson's life failed to find a publisher, but she completed it shortly before her death in 1994, and it is available to readers in the University Archives at Butler's Irwin Library in Indianapolis.

Happily, Ray E. Boomhower of the Indiana Historical Society, the editor of the Indiana Historical Society Press's Indiana Biography Series, has given me a second chance to do a Nicholson study. I am grateful to him and others at the IHS Press, especially Rachel M. Popma, for this opportunity. The author also appreciates the services of countless librarians, archivists, and curators who eased his study of relevant Nicholson materials. Finally, I want to recognize again in print the enormous assistance—as fellow researcher, critic, copy editor, and typist—of my wife, Beth Van Vorst Gray. An avid reader and writer herself, she has become a real fan of "Nick," and her support during the life of this project has been splendid.

1

Old Familiar Faces

*"Every well-regulated family should have a grandfather within call,
to participate in all ceremonies and festivities and for his consolatory
value in hours of adversity."*[1]

MEREDITH NICHOLSON, 1929

"MY ATTACHMENTS ARE ALL LOCAL, PURELY LOCAL. I HAVE NO
passion (or have had none since I was in love . . .) to groves
and vallies. The rooms where I was born, the furniture
which has been before my eyes all my life—a bookcase
. . . , old chairs, old tables, streets, squares, where I have
sunned myself, my old school—these are my mistresses."
These lines written by Charles Lamb to William Words-
worth in 1801 were used by Meredith Nicholson to open
his last book, a collection of essays titled *Old Familiar
Faces* (1929), which in turn opened with a largely autobiographical chapter, "One's Grandfather." Here we learn
most of what is known about Nicholson's forebears, the
Nicholsons and the Merediths. The author was enormously proud of the fact that both ancestral lines had
Celtic influences, to which he attributed his love of music
and poetry, and had come to America long before the
American Revolution.

More is known about the Merediths, given their greater involvement in public affairs, than the Nicholsons, who represented an unbroken line of tillers of the soil until Meredith Nicholson carved out new endeavors for himself. Nicholson's great-grandfather, John Wheeler Meredith, a swashbuckling merchant-seaman of Welsh origins, was a native of Delaware who was in the Caribbean when the Revolutionary War began. On his way home, he was wounded during a naval battle, recovered, and joined in the uprising, eventually serving under General George Washington. He subsequently married and moved to Pennsylvania, where the Merediths soon welcomed a son, Samuel Caldwell, into their midst. This enterprising young man, the main character in Nicholson's chapter on grandfathers, also lived in Ohio before moving to Centerville, Indiana, in 1834, serving as editor and publisher of various Whig newspapers in the 1830s and 1840s.[2]

After purchasing an "old printing office" from the estate of Septimus Smith, Meredith issued the first number of *The People's Advocate* on January 6, 1835, changing the paper's name and its politics (from Democrat to Whig) a year later. But Meredith sold the paper, renamed the *Wayne County Chronicle*, in 1839 and lived briefly in Illinois and Iowa before returning to Centerville in late 1840. In January 1841 he began publishing the *Wayne County Record*. In 1848, however, he sold the paper, moved to Indianapolis, and worked in the offices of the *Indianapolis Journal*. Shortly thereafter news about the discovery of gold in California stirred his emotions and he became a forty-niner. Leaving home in October 1849 with two friends from Hagerstown, Indiana, Meredith traveled first to Panama and then sailed aboard the misnamed *Sea Queen*, finally arriving in San Francisco after a difficult monthlong voyage on January 11, 1850. Eschewing the prospector's life, Meredith instead did odd jobs before landing work as a printer for $60 a week (and later as much as $121 weekly), probably more than most of the prospectors earned.

Meredith remained in California only nine months, preferring life in the more settled environment of central Indiana, a state that was just then emerging from its pioneer period. He resumed his printing trade in Indianapolis, where he lived into his nineties, some of the time with his daughter's family that included young Meredith Nicholson. The future author found it difficult to believe the balding, mild-mannered man, who was never without reading material as he sat in his favorite easy chair in the evening, had actually been a daring forty-niner, but he had the old gentleman's penciled-in diary to prove it. The document was one of the grandson's prized possessions in his later days.

Less is known about the early Nicholsons of Scotch-Irish heritage, who migrated to North Carolina and then moved to Virginia and Kentucky. At least we know that a Nicholson, the author's great-grandfather, fought in the Revolutionary War, farmed in Virginia and Kentucky, and is buried in Crab Orchard, Kentucky, a small village in Lincoln County, one of the three original counties in the state. Meredith Nicholson visited the ancestral grave at least once, perhaps while en route to Tennessee to conduct research for a major historical novel on the early (prepresidential) life of Andrew Jackson titled *The Cavalier of Tennessee* (1928). A son, James, the author's grandfather, was born in Crab Orchard and, like his father, was a farmer. James and his wife, Elizabeth Willis Nicholson, eventually migrated to Decatur, Illinois, where James had received a land grant for his military service under General Arthur St. Clair in the 1780s and where he died at the age of ninety-one. It is also believed that Nicholson's paternal great-grandmother was from County Cork, Ireland, although that may have been the port from which she sailed rather than her home.

The author's father, Edward Willis Nicholson, was born in the early 1830s in Kentucky and grew up on the family farm with his six siblings—two brothers and four sisters. When Edward was ready to strike out on his own sometime in the 1850s, he moved to Montgomery County, Indiana, and started farming there.

Nothing is known of his attitudes and concerns as the clouds of war gathered in the South, but as soon as Fort

IHS, BASS PHOTO COMPANY COLLECTION

*Etching of the Eleventh Indiana in action during
the Civil War in Romney, Virginia.*

Sumter was fired upon and Indiana governor Oliver P.
Morton called for volunteers, Nicholson was among the
hundreds of young men who answered the call, although
he was older than most. On April 18, 1861, already a
member of the Zouave Regiment commanded by Colonel
Lew Wallace of Crawfordsville, Nicholson and his fellow
soldiers joined the Union army as the Indiana Eleventh
Volunteer Regiment for ninety days, the maximum then
possible. He served with the Zouaves in western Virginia, the scene of fierce early battles. Following his reen-
listment for three years as an officer in a light artillery

company, the Indiana Ninth Battery, Sergeant Nicholson participated in the horrendous Battle of Shiloh in April 1862, "the bloodiest single battle in the West," according to Indiana historian Emma Lou Thornbrough. Nicholson survived the battle, but extended exposure afterwards in wet weather without blankets or tents (which had been abandoned at Crump's Landing when, as his commanding officer reported, "the Command was ordered to march to Shiloh") led to prolonged illness and chronic diarrhea. Nevertheless, after recuperating for several weeks in Indianapolis, he returned to active duty in July 1862, this time as a lieutenant, then captain of the Indiana Twenty-second Battery, from which he was discharged on July 7, 1865.[3]

The good aspect of Edward Nicholson's unpleasant odyssey through the war years was that he met a nurse, Emily Ellen Meredith, Samuel C. Meredith's daughter, during his recuperation, and they continued seeing each other when the war ended. On November 1, 1865, the young couple was married in Indianapolis by the Reverend F. C. Holliday. Soon thereafter the Nicholsons set up housekeeping in Crawfordsville, where just thirteen months later, on December 9, 1866, they became the proud parents of a son, who was named for both parents—Willis Meredith Nicholson. In fact, the lad used both given names for a while, and his first published book of poetic "songs," as he termed them, carried the byline of Will Meredith Nicholson. He also gloried in the fact that his birthday coincided with that of John Milton and believed he was destined to become a writer.

Never fully recovering from the illness he contracted during the Civil War, Edward Nicholson was unable to perform true manual labor and instead had a series of low-paying jobs. For a time, as listed in pension records, he was a merchant and then a police officer. Finally, he secured a place as "superintendent" of something in Washington, D.C., really a sinecure, to which he traveled alone and remained there, apart from his family, for six or seven years. It might be said that Captain Nicholson, in August 1894, became one of the last victims of the Civil War, for he died in the nation's capital by his own hand. The District of Columbia Department of Health's death certificate simply lists the cause of death as a "gunshot wound penetrating [the] heart (suicidal hemorrhage)." The family was deeply shocked and saddened at the news, but also relieved to know that Nicholson's years of pain and suffering were over, and his son never ceased to honor his father's memory and to be proud of his service to his country.[4]

Very little else is known about the author's relationship with his father. The few references to the man in Nicholson's writings reveal warm feelings toward him. He noted that his father was "the gentlest of men; he met failure and disappointment with a brave spirit." Earlier, in responding on black-lined stationery to a letter of condolence in

1894, Nicholson told close friend May Shipp that, as only she had seemed to realize, "my father was to me a link between our peaceful day and the war; [and] that through him I feel tenderly toward all men who were participators in the great conflict."[5]

2

Without Benefit of College

"A narrative of personal experience is worthless unless it is true, and this story of the processes by which I gained what may be called an education is as frank and accurate as I can make it. I shouldn't be writing it at all if it were not for the hope that some boy or girl, denied an opportunity to go to college . . . may find comfort and encouragement in my confessions."[1]

MEREDITH NICHOLSON, 1926

A WRITING CAREER SEEMED AS UNLIKELY FOR THE CHUBBY little boy from Crawfordsville as an athletic or an operatic career. Meredith Nicholson was, he knew, unsuited for any such activity, but he did in time aspire to emulate his grandfather and an uncle who were printers, a seemingly glamorous and adventuresome occupation. Clearly the life of a husbandman, or farmer, had no appeal for the young Nicholson, and the opportunity (or the necessity) to work in the field alongside his father disappeared when his father had to abandon his first calling for reasons of health. In 1872 the Nicholson family, now numbering four upon the birth of Margaret in 1870, moved to Indianapolis, where the elder Nicholson hoped to find indoor employment. Young Meredith, only five years old at the time of the move, retained just dim memories of living in Crawfordsville, one of which was the frequent haunting but beguiling sounds of a bugle at sundown, evidently the refrains of an unknown Civil War veteran that came wafting through the hillside breezes. The boy also delighted in the fact that Crawfordsville was the home of Wabash College, an institution he never attended but developed close associations with, and he was enormously proud of Crawfordsville's many talented writers at the end of the century, people such as the Thompson brothers, Maurice and Will; the Krout sisters, Mary and Caroline; and of course, the incomparable and world-famous Lew Wallace and his wife, Susan, also a writer. Wallace's fame rested primarily upon his book, *Ben-Hur: A Tale of the Christ* (1880), but he was also a distinguished Mexican and Civil War officer who later became the American minister to Turkey, appointed by President James A. Garfield.[2]

These fleeting connections and associations with people and institutions of greatness in his hometown faded as Nicholson faced a new life in the capital city. He and his family moved into a house next door to his grandfather Meredith, the former newspaper publisher and editor, who then plied his trade for others. The Meredith and Nicholson homes were located on Blackford Street, on Indianapolis's near west side just beyond the boundaries of the city's original Mile Square. The houses were also near the White River, where Nicholson passed many happy hours playing on the banks, occasionally fishing, but never learning to swim.

When it was time to enroll in school, Nicholson attended the Fourth Ward School, also on Blackford Street

IHS, LEW WALLACE COLLECTION, M292

Lew Wallace, former Civil War general and author of Ben-Hur.

a few blocks to the north of his home. But it was not a happy experience. Although he wanted to learn and loved to read, he was not comfortable with the routine and the discipline required by his teachers. He was embarrassed that his mother had to confer frequently with his teachers in an effort to find ways to help her son be successful in his studies. Emily Nicholson was an educated woman, having attended college in both Centerville and Indianapolis. An omnivorous reader just like her father, she attended as many cultural events in the city—public lectures, concerts, civic celebrations—as possible. Usually young Meredith went with his mother, and he often recalled with fondness and gratitude his chances to hear such famous people as Mark Twain and George Washington Cable speak. He was especially impressed when his father, usually not heavily involved in the boy's education, took him downtown on the occasion of his thirteenth birthday, December 9, 1879, and introduced the boy to General Ulysses S. Grant, then just concluding a world tour, who cordially shook the hand of his fellow soldier's offspring. Nicholson reflected late in his own life that he might be the only living Hoosier who had shaken the hand of the Civil War hero and president. He also once trotted through the streets alongside the carriage of General William T. Sherman when the hero of the Atlanta campaign visited Indianapolis. Nicholson had a particularly warm spot in his heart for Sherman, with whom his father had served and to whom people said he bore a resemblance.[3]

Nicholson often wrote short autobiographical pieces about his childhood and his lack of a formal education beyond grammar school. The most extensive such essay, whose title is used at the head of this chapter and which might instead have been "Without Benefit of High School," was not a boast about having skipped both high school and college, but was intended as a moral to others, especially parents concerned about their poorly educated children. At the end of the nineteenth century, one need not, as Nicholson's life abundantly indicated, receive a formal higher education in order to succeed in life. But, as his life also indicated, a vibrant imagination and an insatiable curiosity, combined with self-imposed industry and study, could lead one into the society of learned people.[4]

Despite his "inability to adjust . . . to the educational machinery" and "panic over the algebraic signs," Nicholson credited "the talk at home" and the way his family connected with American history—the Revolutionary War, the Gold Rush, the Civil War, current social and political issues—with kindling in him "a keen curiosity as to all things of contemporaneous human interest." His mother, who Nicholson declared had "much better educational advantages than my father and . . . a much broader range of interests" and "political prejudices [that] were the strongest I have ever known," particularly sparked his own interest in learning and spawned his lifelong sensitivity to feminist issues and women's rights, as revealed in many of his novels with robust female characters. He fondly recalled his mother's frequent reference to a comment by a Quaker friend who had said "she'd never lie straight in her coffin unless she voted before she died." Happily, Emily Nicholson herself, although she died before the Nineteenth Amendment (adopted in 1920) established women's suffrage in Indiana, was able "to exercise the right of franchise once though she had to establish her citizenship in Colorado to do it!"[5]

One might say that, more so than for most who made the claim, Nicholson was truly a self-educated, self-made man. That education, so painful and frustrating in a schoolhouse, was accomplished through omnivorous reading wherever and whenever possible, beginning with his grandfather's newspapers and magazines. Later, novels by James Fenimore Cooper and William Gilmore Simms, plays and poems by William Shakespeare, the Bible, and the Book of Common Prayer formed the core of Nicholson's eclectic, serendipitous reading. The influences of these works can often be found in his writing, including his informal correspondence, often punctuated, like the Psalms, with the word "Selah" after an important pronouncement or especially interesting phraseology.

Another newcomer to the city of Indianapolis in the early 1870s, in addition to the Nicholsons, was the Indianapolis Public Library. Established first in the Robert Underhill home at the corner of Michigan and Pennsylvania streets in the building that also served as the second home of the Indianapolis High School, the library moved in 1876 to the second floor of the Sentinel Building in the heart of downtown Indianapolis. In this location, Nicholson frequented the reading room, the windows of which overlooked the Circle, not yet the site of the magnificent Soldiers and Sailors Monument erected there in the 1890s, but then just Circle Park. "On hot summer days," Nicholson remembered, "I used to go to the library . . . get me an Oliver Optic, a Mayme Reid, or a Henry Castleman and lie under a tree in the park and read." In 1880

IHS, BASS PHOTO COMPANY COLLECTION, P130

The Great Room of Indianapolis's central library.

the library moved to Alvord House, at the intersection of Pennsylvania and Ohio streets, and a dozen years later moved again to a new home at Ohio and Meridian streets. A final move occurred in 1917, when a remarkable new library was erected on St. Clair Street between Meridian and Pennsylvania streets. Nicholson continued his close relationship with the library in all its locations, including the new one. On March 24, 1916, when the city celebrated laying the library's cornerstone near land donated by James Whitcomb Riley, Nicholson delivered the main address to the hundreds of guests in attendance. Sadly, Riley himself was not well enough to attend—he died later that year— but one thousand school children sang Riley's "Messiah of the Nation," especially written for the occasion, to music composed by John Philip Sousa. Nicholson also served on a contentious library committee that selected the names of seventy-six literary men and women that were to adorn the stonework above the windows, both inside and outside.[6]

The first librarian of the Indianapolis Public Library, Charles Evans, later established himself as a world-famous bibliographer, and he recalled in 1927 that upon his daily walks to work he passed the Nicholson home. He "some-times would see a small boy with large wondering eyes, swinging on the wooden gate of the fence surrounding it, and shyly gazing at the passersby. We never spoke. But that is the early picture memory holds of Meredith Nicholson, upon whom, in my judgment has fallen the mantle so long and worthily worn by William D. Howells, as Dean of American Men of Letters."[7]

Such accolades, common in Nicholson's later years, were hardly anticipated by the unschooled lad who was soon forced to begin earning his own way in the world. The first money (twenty-five cents) young Meredith ever earned was in 1876, when he was hired one evening by a newsman to rush telegraphic dispatches to the newspaper office about Rutherford B. Hayes's nomination for the presidency, which culminated in Hayes's victory in the momentous and disputed election of that year. These errands kept Nicholson busy until about 2:00 a.m., and upon returning home, he encountered the members of his family who were about to set off in search of the "missing" boy. Although chagrined at the unnecessary worry he had given his parents, undoubtedly it had appealed to Nicholson's sense of importance (and history) to play even a minor role in reporting this political event. It also marked the first time he had seen reporters at work, and that heightened his resolve to become one.[8]

Nicholson's main part-time job while still in school was working at a soda fountain for two summers. Upon realizing that, despite his best efforts, school just "didn't fit" him, in the midst of his freshman year in high school he abruptly quit and sought employment as a printer. "To be a 'print,'" he rationalized, "and wander the world, holding cases in strange cities struck me as a noble thing." And he did find a job at a small print shop attached to a newsstand, where he could, in his spare time, "read Bonner's Ledger, and the newest dime novels." Nicholson's position was that of a clerk, however, not an apprentice. Rarely did he "get a chance to sort pi or otherwise toy with the type," so he moved on to a larger printing office where, although his salary doubled, from $1 to $2 a week, he was thwarted again. The work consisted mainly of pushing a wobbly wheelbarrow, heavily loaded with books and papers, over the cobblestone streets and countless railroad tracks in downtown Indianapolis. Moreover, at seven each morning, in Nicholson's euphemistic phrasing, "I gained spiritual strength for this task by sweeping out the counting room and administering to the cuspidors."

Inspired by his dissatisfaction at being an errand boy and janitor in print shops, Nicholson, with a friend, took up the study of shorthand and "practiced the pothooks" (his word for the appearance of shorthand strokes). Intrigued by the odd-sounding Latin words he often encountered in this work, he began the study of Latin, then French and German, even Greek, too, and at this time he also began to write. Soon, his skills in stenography and his fluency in languages led to his "emancipation from the wheelbarrow" and helped him find a position with a court reporter. Still an errand boy and still earning $2 a week, Nicholson began taking dictation from the reporter between sessions of the court, and in time he was ready to take depositions and fill in for lawyers "in need of special secretarial help."[9]

In time this introduction into the arcana of the legal world led to Nicholson accepting a position in the law offices of John T. Dye and William P. Fishback. Later, in a fortuitous step, he moved on to the law office of William Wallace, the younger brother of Lew Wallace. He was thrilled when this permitted occasional meetings with the famed author upon his return from Turkey in 1885; Nicholson always "felt his charm." Though born in Indiana and the son of an Indiana governor, Wallace "was not like other Hoosier folk. Swarthy as an Arab, gracious but incisive of speech, he struck me always as just having arrived, forthright and bent upon adventure, from some far land of enchantment." Wallace, who made the law office "his loafing place" during visits to Indianapolis, consented to look over the verses Nicholson timidly "offered for his criticism" and he "spoke encouragingly" to Nicholson about them. The worldly Wallace also corrected Nicholson's pronunciation of the word Italian, "when I used it in his presence with the initial i long!"[10]

His experiences in both law offices awakened in Nicholson an awareness of life beyond his own limited circle. Attorneys Dye and Fishback "were cultivated men, with a wide range of interests," and through them Nicholson "began to realize the existence of such a thing as an intellectual life. There were forces and tendencies in the world that I had never dreamed of. The cultivated thinking men of the city dropped into the office, and I heard there first the names of Darwin, Huxley, John Stuart Mill and the rest of the great Victorians." Nicholson also became interested in politics at the time of the heated campaign between James G. Blaine, Republican presidential hopeful, and Democrat Grover Cleveland, the reform mayor of Buffalo, New York, in 1884. Like the attorneys in his office,

Republicans all, who "promptly turned Mugwump" at this point, so did the young Nicholson, even though his family was "strongly Republican." Clearly doubting the qualifications of the "Plumed Knight" to be president, Nicholson became an ardent Cleveland supporter and remained a Democrat throughout his life, even though his mother, who suspected the party of harboring Confederate sympathizers during the Civil War, resented the shift in her son's partisanship.

Nicholson's learning, and his writing, continued when he switched to the Wallace law office. He was even permitted to appear in court on minor business for the firm. Encouraged "to take up the law in earnest," he did considerable background reading and, upon discovering there was such a thing as maritime law, "went after it with enthusiasm, searching out all the cases in the reports, as much for the 'stories' of collisions and other causes of action incident to those who go down to the sea in ships as for the point of the decisions." This smattering of legal learning served him well in his subsequent writing.[11]

As Nicholson noted at the time, "nothing troubled me very much . . . except my ignorance!" Rather than returning to school, he kept on pursuing self-education activities with a vengeance. "What others knew I wanted to know," he said, and he believed it was "sheer good luck that threw me with men of cultivation at that period," from whom he learned enormously. Realizing that he would never have succeeded in college and its "routine of a fixed curricu-lum," Nicholson instead gathered "such fruit as pleased me from the tree of knowledge and did not worry about the rest." He insisted that he had "the greatest reverence for established scholarship, but I was born with what, I believe, is called a journalistic mind and took the shortest cut to any information I wanted."[12]

Among Nicholson's "teachers" in his chosen way of life were a number of notable characters on the Indianapolis scene. These idiosyncratic individuals included newspaper-men Colonel W. R. Holloway and Berry R. Sulgrove, min-isters O. C. McCulloch and Myron W. Reed, and the last of the "cloaked poets" who roamed the streets of Indianapolis: Benjamin D. House, a brilliant, eccentric poet and Civil War veteran from Vermont who settled in Indianapolis after the war, and Daniel L. Paine. Reed, an iconoclastic Presbyterian minister, was a particular favorite and role model for the impressionable Nicholson. Reed was strikingly handsome, tall and dark, and his sermons, with their casual references to Ralph Waldo Emerson and Henry David Thoreau, were so appealing that Nicholson and a friend would regularly "attach" themselves "to the back seat of Reed's church"; lis-ten to the minister, standing "straight and tall in his pulpit," read his "Emerson-like essay" sermons; and then sneak out "fearful lest someone would speak to us."[13]

Another person who contributed mightily to Nichol-son's learning and to his growing sense of self-worth was

James Whitcomb Riley.

James Whitcomb Riley, who had visited the law office seeking out the author of some lines of verse that had appeared in a Cincinnati newspaper, reprinted from an Indianapolis paper. When Nicholson realized that Riley—"a poet of mounting fame at that time"—knew of his "presence on the earth," it lifted his spirits "to a new high altitude." A few days later Riley returned to show Nicholson some poems he was getting together for a book, and the two went out for dinner that evening. Riley ordered them beefsteak with mushrooms, Nicholson's "first acquaintance with that delectable combination," and an unending if unlikely warm friendship began. What helped Nicholson the most at first was Riley's "generous assumption that I was a writer. He wrote and I wrote. We were both writers!" He concluded that he owed an "incalculable" debt to Riley. Perhaps the greatest lesson learned was that "a writer serves himself best by using home material." This Nicholson never forgot and practiced always. Even after his service abroad, when friends urged that he do a novel set in Latin America, he deflected their suggestions with the mantra, "Write about what you know."[14]

It was a natural progression for the young poet-in-waiting in a law office to get a job as a writer as soon as possible. That opportunity arose in the summer of 1886 when the ownership of the *Indianapolis Sentinel* changed. Its new editor, Gus C. Matthews of Chicago, was already known to the Nicholsons. An old friend of Edward

Nicholson, Matthews previously edited *The Current Magazine* in Chicago and had accepted for publication a few of young Nicholson's poems. Thus, when looking about for a reporter for the morning paper, Matthews and Scott C. Bone, the city editor, hired Nicholson at the princely sum (or so it seemed to the young man at the time) of $12 a week. Nicholson had been earning $7 weekly. But the new working hours, from noon until 2:30 a.m. when the presses rolled, left much to be desired.[15]

3

The Poet

Like the dreamland visions
I have caught of you,
Or the unvoiced songs that
I have wrought of you
Is the breath of Spring that
Fills my thought of you![1]

MEREDITH NICHOLSON, 1893

INDIANAPOLIS TRANSFORMED ITSELF DURING THE LAST QUARTER of the nineteenth century from a raw frontier town to a large industrialized city. Established in the 1820s in the center of the new state of Indiana, where the state capital would be relocated in 1825, the city was not modernized until, beginning in the 1870s, street and road improvements, a vast expansion of the state's railroad network centered in Indianapolis, and the creation of such basic city utilities as a water works, professional fire and police departments, and an urban transport system occurred. Additionally, major public buildings, some of which still adorn the cityscape, were constructed. These included a new state capitol (1888); a new city hall (1876, but since replaced); a home (1893) for the Commercial Club (later known as the Chamber of Commerce); a number of theaters and private clubs, especially Das Deutsche Haus (1890s), now known as the Athenaeum; and, finally and most dramatically, the Soldiers and Sailors Monument (1888–1901), generally considered the finest Civil War monument in the nation. In his popular history of the city, Edward Leary called the period of the 1880s and 1890s "Oh, Those Golden Years," and Claude Bowers, a journalist, political leader, and diplomat who spent his boyhood in Indianapolis, called the late nineteenth century the "city's springtime."[2]

By 1890 the city boasted of a population of more than 100,000 and a number of substantial industrial companies, such as Kingan & Company, a large meatpacking firm; a huge stockyard; the Indianapolis Manufacturing Company, then the nation's biggest producer of baby carriages; and the Parry Manufacturing Company, which operated "the world's largest cart-, wagon- and carriage-making plant."[3] Nicholson and his family had come to the capital city in time to witness this transformation, and Nicholson helped report on it as a newspaperman for about a dozen years. After one year with the *Indianapolis Sentinel*, Nicholson spent another eleven years at the *Indianapolis News*.

As a cub reporter, Nicholson's first assignment with the *Sentinel* from city editor Scott C. Bone was on the police and courthouse beats. There he quickly learned a great deal about the underlife of his adopted city, but he also learned the craft of his business. Bone complimented his

IHS, BASS PHOTO COMPANY COLLECTION, P130

Soldiers and Sailors Monument, Indianapolis.

young protégé, not yet twenty years old when he became a reporter, calling him a "fine fellow" who, he predicted, "would do well in the future." When Nicholson moved on to the *News*, he sat, over the years, at virtually every editorial desk in the company.[4]

One of Nicholson's most memorable assignments as a reporter with the *News* was to cover the "tally sheet" scandal in 1887–88 that involved the inimitable Simeon Coy, the owner of two saloons in Indianapolis and the chairman of the Democratic Party in Marion County. Coy (1851–94) was a saloon keeper after 1875 and a member of the Indianapolis City Council from 1878 to 1886. He was elected chairman of the Marion County Democratic Party in 1884 and was reelected in 1886. In 1887 Coy and eleven others were accused of tampering with election returns. Indicted in May 1887 and tried, first in July 1887 and again in January 1888, Coy served a short prison term while remaining on the city council, to which he was reelected upon his release from prison in October 1889. That same year he published his own lengthy account of the case, *The Great Conspiracy*—the "conspiracy" being on the part of the Republicans to taint Democrats.[5]

As Nicholson recalled this episode in 1936 while serving as the United States Minister in Venezuela,

I reported the proceedings for The News and recall vividly the appearance of Mr. Justice [John M.] Harlan, who was a very large man, with a big bald head which became scarlet as the arguments went on. The federal contention was sustained and Coy and Bernhamer, and perhaps others of the indictees, went to prison. I knew Coy well in his

38

better days, when he owned two excellent saloons and was otherwise a colorful, amusing individual. He was most beautifully, magnificently illiterate but had a gift for droll sayings, as for example, "When I'm done I'm did." While in prison he studied the Bible assiduously and upon emerging wrote a book, no doubt with the assistance of a ghost writer, and thus joined our Hoosier literary group.[6]

During his years as a reporter, Nicholson continued to learn and to grow, and to write poetry in his spare time. Indeed, this was his main ambition, and he worked at it steadily, but gained little except for a growing local reputation. The local papers that printed Nicholson's verses, usually poems of either four or eight lines, did not remunerate the author, and the few times he placed his "songs" in national journals, such as *The Century* (edited in Boston) or *Harper's* (New York), the compensation was rarely more than $3 or $5 for each contribution.

There are only a few known examples of Nicholson's early editorials, book reviews, and news stories, most of his writing being without attribution. But in 1890, shortly after transferring to the *News*, he spoke out in favor of an international copyright law which, he said, "for the sake of common honesty," should be passed. "To steal or not to steal, that is the question," said Nicholson. He said that its defeat in Congress had besmirched the country's reputation and that the bill should be reconsidered and adopted.[7]

More dramatically and more pleasing to Nicholson's ambitions was the featured (and signed) front-page poem he wrote welcoming an estimated one hundred thousand Union army veterans to the twenty-seventh Grand Army of the Republic convention, which in 1893 was being held in Indianapolis for the third time. Nicholson cast this "Song of Welcome" in the form of a statement from torch-bearing *Miss Indiana*, the statue atop the still-incomplete Civil War monument on the Circle, but the sentiments expressed were clearly the author's own, too. Both of his parents were, in a sense, Civil War veterans. The second stanza set the tone of the message:

> O ye who from the farthest shore
>> Of this broad land assemble here,
> We hold you, as our country, dear—
>> The city and its heart are yours."

The twelve-stanza composition ended with these words:

> And by my torch, new-lit, and its bright glow,
>> Whose rays the triumphs of brave progress show,
> I echo, "Welcome, Saviors of the Land!"[8]

Nicholson's first poem in the *News* had appeared earlier, on November 19, 1885, and he had dozens of them published there and in the *Indianapolis Journal* by 1890. His first publications, however, were poems in the *Crawfordsville Journal* in the first half of 1885, and he placed other "songs" in a number of newspapers and magazines outside of Indiana. It is interesting to note that his first lines to see print were a Civil War poem, "1861–1865," carried by his hometown newspaper on January 24, 1885. This was followed by "A Bit of History" and four other poems that appeared by June 1885. His first Indianapolis newspaper entries began in July of that year and continued regularly, even during Nicholson's years as a businessman, until his primary writing shifted to prose near the turn of the century.[9]

Based upon these early publications and, probably, the young man's acquaintances with authors James Whitcomb Riley and Lew Wallace, and attorneys William P. Fishback and John T. Dye, Nicholson was invited to join the prestigious Indianapolis Literary Club in 1889. Established in 1877 by Charles Evans and others and modeled upon the Literary Club of Cincinnati, the Indianapolis club's membership was practically a roster of the city's most influential men, including even the sitting president of the United States, Benjamin Harrison. Nicholson was flattered at the invitation and eagerly accepted, but he mildly scandalized some of the conservative intellects gathered there when he read his first paper to them. It dealt with the life and poetry of the flamboyant Walt Whitman, not considered a worthy subject by all. Nevertheless, Nicholson remained a member in good standing and took increasing pride (and leadership roles) in his associations with other literary men of Indianapolis.[10]

Although Nicholson's book, *The Poet* (1914), was a tribute to, not a biography of, James Whitcomb Riley, its title nevertheless serves as a description of Nicholson's early years of manhood. As noted above, all of his first publications, apart from a $10 prize-winning essay, "Tale of a Postage Stamp," that appeared in the *Chicago Tribune* on February 20, 1886, were verses, and his first book, *Short Flights* (1891), was a collection of some sixty items, most of which had previously come out in the local press. As Nicholson later wrote in the copy owned by the local library, these verses "were written between my seventeenth and twenty-second year," beginning, that is, just shortly after he had dropped out of school. Nicholson was justly proud of his poems and valued the training and discipline that resulted. "Versifying is an excellent preparation for prose," he told an aspiring young English teacher in 1925, "as it gives practice in precision and brevity."[11]

He also gained his earliest statewide and national recognition as a poet. *Poets and Poetry of Indiana* (1900), a large hardcover anthology of the best work of dozens of Hoosier-based writers, included perhaps the first published biographical sketch of Nicholson. "Mr. Nicholson," according to the editors, "is rapidly winning a high position among American poets." This collection, which even carried a photograph of Nicholson, used five of his poems. Riley, not yet an iconic figure, had but six, second only to Benjamin D. House's seven. Nicholson, who admired House, edited a collection of his writings complete with a biographical sketch in 1892.[12]

When he was not engaged in versifying, Nicholson devoted himself to journalism and to a limited social life. Although his politics coincided more with the Democratic *Sentinel*, his personal life was more in tune with the time-table of the *News*, a conservative Republican paper, which had mid-morning or later deadlines. This left the aspiring youth with his evenings free, mainly for reading and writing and for attendance at a growing number of cultural programs (and a few entertainments). According to Nicholson, however, he knew nothing about social life until age twenty-three or twenty-four. "I knew no girls except my sister's friends; I attended only two or three parties in my school-days but didn't enjoy them particularly," he noted. "I was too busy for that sort of thing—too busy even to get into mischief!"[13]

Nicholson, now a tall, handsome young man, still very shy and totally inexperienced in dealing with the opposite sex, was nevertheless an appealing young man very much in demand as a speaker or reader of his own works. At least once in these early years, he returned to Crawfordsville to speak to a church group. In time he developed friendships

in Indianapolis with other similarly inclined would-be professional writers, including May and Margaret Shipp, state
historian Jacob Piatt Dunn Jr., editor Hewitt H. Howland, and, most notably perhaps, Booth Tarkington, who
in contrast to Nicholson, came from the "high society" of
Indianapolis. "Tark" was also a bit younger than Nicholson
and, like him, was not a college graduate, although he had
attended both Purdue and Princeton universities, where
he excelled in extracurricular activities such as helping
write and perform in the annual student musicals. Tarkington's goal to be a novelist was clear, but he, unlike Nicholson, ran into trouble trying to get his first book published.
Nicholson later quietly commented that he never had a
book manuscript, not even his first one, turned down by
a publisher, but admitted to collecting "pink slips" (rejec-
tions) by the hundreds for his poems.

Nicholson also made friends, something he did easily,
with young businessmen and up-and-coming activists on
the Indianapolis scene. Some of these comrades lived in
Woodruff Place, one of Indianapolis's first suburbs on the
city's eastside connected by streetcar with the downtown.
Nicholson also was frequently a guest in the homes of
Alfred Potts, whom he also visited in Culver at his home
on Lake Maxinkuckee; John Griffiths, referred to by Nicholson as a "distinguished orator, afterward consul-general
in London"; and William Fortune, whose "charming wife"
Nicholson said, quoting some favorite lines, was "divinely

IHS, C6017

Indiana author and politician Booth Tarkington.

tall and most divinely fair." Fortune, like Nicholson, had begun his career in the city as a newspaperman, and he later established his reputation as a founder of the Commercial Club and the Indianapolis chapter of the Red Cross. In particular, too, Nicholson was a good friend of "the demure Miss [May] Shipp," a talented writer and editor for whom the lines quoted above at the beginning of this chapter were intended. As a friend to editor Shipp and a poet eager for publication, he regularly contributed verses to her annual *Flower Mission Magazine*. Intended as a fund-raiser for the Flower Mission Society, organized in 1892 to assist the indigent and particularly sick children, the magazine offered prose and poetry from an amazing number of future well-known writers. Sharing space with Nicholson in the early issues of the short-lived magazine were two others of the so-called Big Four of Indiana writers (Riley and Tarkington) as well as many more.[14]

Widely scattered letters by Nicholson from his years as a reporter and a poet give some indication of his activities and suggest brief flirtations with one or two young women. His activities included giving a few talks on subjects unknown, but probably these focused on readings of his poetry. In 1891 he wrote to a married friend, Mary Jameson Judah, worried that he had "come across badly" as a gossip on their drive and offered, perhaps as penance, to fill in for another "lecturer." Nicholson was willing "to come myself and give a parlor talk on 'A Dear Little Hoosier Sweetheart, with smoky eyes and the peace of holy angels in her heart!'"[15] Unfortunately, the identity of that "sweetheart" is not known but might have been Shipp.

In 1892 Nicholson again confided in Judah his discontent with the way his life was going: "The day is cold

and dark and dreary and dusty for the rain that would fall
into every life cometh not, and my life, too, is parched and
dusty, and the leaves go tumbling down into it in the most
melancholy fashion . . . . She has come home again. She
is the most charming, the most beautiful of women." He
apologized for saying unkind, wicked things about her and
wondered why he had done so. Perhaps it was "because I
cared for her so much and hated myself for it!" Then he
lapsed into a "Song," a long lament with the refrain, "O
Life! O Love!":

Between the daffodils and goldenrod
A myriad flowers have lined the paths I trod
When life and love made glad the fallen clod
O life! O love!
From Spring's first flowers and Autumn's blighted leaf
I was unvisited by doubt and grief
For love and life were all of my belief—
O life! O love!

The summer flowers have tangled in the mold,
After the twilight winds blew sharp and cold—
But life fails not while love keeps firm its hold—
O life! O love!

He continued, "If I had more sense—some sense—things
would not be as they are. My situation is that of a man who

has followed a light for a long time and abandoned the pursuit just as he was about to realize and secure O Life! O Love!" He closed this unusual letter noting that he and "the demure Miss Shipp" (clearly not the lady who had "just come home") went to hear "the Orators" the other night, one of whom was New Yorker Chauncey Depew, who kept them "spellbound." "How charming this same demure young woman . . . . Ah me! Those days at Maxinkuckee—It wrenches my heart to think of them."[16]

This reference to Lake Maxinkuckee, near Culver in northern Indiana, later to be used as the setting in his most famous novel, *The House of a Thousand Candles*, may have come following Nicholson's first trip to that spot. Now in his midtwenties, Nicholson was becoming worldlier and better traveled. He mentioned several times not having seen an ocean until after he was a voter, but not long after turning twenty-one Nicholson traveled to Boston and probably New York, too. In these publishing centers, Nicholson sought out the editors of magazines to which he had contributed some verses and perhaps delivered more. His long friendship with Indiana-bred Robert Underwood Johnson, the long-tenured editor of *Century Magazine* and one of those responsible for bringing into print the monumental *Battles and Leaders of the Civil War* (1884–88), dates from such a visit.[17]

Nicholson also had a fateful encounter, perhaps by chance, with Professor George Edward Woodberry in

Cambridge, Massachusetts, in 1891, shortly after Woodberry had read and perhaps reviewed Nicholson's first book of poetry, which he liked very much. Woodberry (1855–1930) at that time had just been appointed to a teaching position at Columbia University, where he went on to an illustrious career as a poet, critic, teacher, and scholar. This meeting was made particularly memorable because, as Nicholson was being given a personal tour by Woodberry of Harvard, his undergraduate college, the professor stumbled and fell at a staircase and Nicholson sprang to his assistance. As he explained some forty years afterwards, Nicholson had "journeyed up to Boston (an adventure in itself) and [Woodberry] met me [there]." When he slipped and fell, "I had to take him to my room and minister to his knee with witch-hazel." Woodberry later referred to Nicholson as his "first pilgrim," and the two poets became lifelong friends.[18]

Nicholson had many close friends at home, too. In addition to his Woodruff Place friends, he was fond of a man referred to only as "Harry," a relative of Booth Tarkington. Nicholson wrote to Harry in 1894: "I am sitting in my room with one eye fastened on your photograph and with the other, of necessity, on this scrap of paper, which is hardly nice enough to bear a message from one gentleman to another, but 'tis all I have. My intentions are honorable, as the fellow says." Nicholson went on to report to Harry that just the evening before he had joined Allen Lewis and

Herbert Painter in the Lewis house and the three of them "said our best things about you, and this took a good deal of time. You can imagine us, three very proper young persons, dressed in their best clothes, watching a decent bit of wood fire—no natural gas nonsense—and talking of you, the world, the flesh and the devil. All the rest of the town was at the Dramatic Club, where it is not likely that the average of pulchritude was as high as it was at the Lewis's." In closing, Nicholson said only a prompt reply to the note would reach him soon, for he had travel plans. "I am meditating flight into a strange land—the land of the Populists—where mails are likely to be intercepted," obviously a reference to a forthcoming trip to Omaha, Nebraska.[19]

Although Nicholson occasionally battled feelings of loneliness and futility, he continued to be a "joiner," remaining active in the city's Dramatic Club, established in 1887 as a women's group and reorganized in 1890 to include men. He had a flair for the dramatic arts and like others, including Tarkington, wrote and acted in some one-act plays. He maintained an active interest in theater throughout his life and once, in collaboration with Kenyon Nicholson (also from Crawfordsville, Indiana, but not a relative), wrote a successful play, *Honor Bright* (1921), based on one of Nicholson's stories of the same name.[20]

Still uncertain and unsure of himself in society, Nicholson, at one point, wrote an abject letter of apology to

Mary Judah, a close friend, who apparently had snubbed him for some unknown reason, obviously an act or word of uncharacteristic rudeness. "I take it all back, every word," a distraught Nicholson pleaded. "I do not know what it was but it must have been something dreadful. Of course, I should not have done it if I had known you would treat me as 'scandalous.' But I am, anyhow, Yours Faithfully."[21]

Showing there was a downside to having one's work appear regularly in the press, Nicholson had "a row" with Tarkington relatives, the Jamesons, over an unintentional slight. As Nicholson explained it to another Jameson, Mary (Jameson) Judah, his "tale of woe" began when the Princeton Glee Club came to Indianapolis and Nicholson was asked on short notice to write about Booth Tarkington, "whom I have loved as a brother, along with all his cousins, aunts, sisters, and mothers." He sent along a clipping of the offending paragraph:

> Newton Booth Tarkington, who is one of the star performers of the Princeton Glee Club, is well-known to many people of Indianapolis—to some as "Booth" and to his intimates as "Tark." The remarkable thing about him so far, next to his refusal to be spoiled, is his capacity for work. An Indianapolis visitor to Princeton was told, a few weeks ago, that "Tark" could put his hand in more things and with better results than anybody else

in the college. This young man was prepared for college at Phillips Exeter, and while at that famous school he learned a great many things and had a vast amount of fun. He rested a year, studying modern languages and making pictures. Then he went to Purdue and studied agriculture for a while. For two years he has been at Princeton, where he has identified himself with all the social expressions of the orange and the black. He is one of the editors of the *Nassau Magazine*, and he is the chief spirit of the *Tiger*, the weekly humorous paper, and a member of the Dramatic and Glee Clubs. The only thing that kept him off the Varsity 'leven this year was the fact that he writes poetry; but it is sensible poetry that wouldn't harm a kitten. Mr. Tarkington's friends sometimes wonder what he will decide to do with himself finally, but all are perfectly confident of his ultimate success, whatever his choice of occupation shall be.[22]

At first Nicholson considered his piece most satisfactory, that it was "good-natured and truthful and all that." But the next morning, "Oh, what a difference." Mrs. Jameson (Booth's aunt) "promptly cut my acquaintance, Mr. Jameson ceased speaking to me and I have been branded as an ass all over town." It was more than a week later before he learned the "row" was over his reference to

Tarkington's poetry. Nicholson "had no idea the boy ever wrote rhymes; if I had dreamed of it I should not have spoken of the sacred gift so breezily." He was most upset that the Jamesons could believe that he had intention-ally belittled their nephew out of jealousy. Nicholson was pleased, however, to learn that Tarkington himself "took it all right and had sense of humor enough to see that the intent of the paragraph was kind." He concluded by expressing his sadness that he had "blindly hurt" when he had "intended to please. I hope you and Mr. Judah won't join the vendetta!"[23]

In what became a life-altering event, Nicholson accepted an invitation to speak at a party given by the Shipp sisters and another Vassar College graduate, Josephine Johnson, in honor of a guest from Omaha, Nebraska. The guest was Eugenie Kountze, a brilliant young woman who, like Johnson and Margaret Shipp, had received a degree from Vassar College (class of 1889) and had been Johnson's roommate there. Kountze had other Indianapolis connections, too. Her grandfather, Thomas Davis, lived there and established a business, the Sinker-Davis Company. For a time, Eugenie had lived with the Davises and attended Indianapolis High School, later known as Shortridge. It is doubtful that Nicholson met Eugenie before the party, but this first meeting led to an instant mutual attraction. Eugenie, an honor student and a member of Phi Beta Kappa whose education included travel abroad, proved to be an ideal match for the self-educated but brilliant reporter eager to make something more of his life.

In short order, Nicholson and Eugenie became good friends. Nicholson even traveled to Omaha in December 1894 to be with Eugenie and to meet the Kountze family. The Kountzes had lived in eastern Nebraska since Herman Kountze, whose German immigrant father had come to Ohio in the 1820s, was sent there by the enterprising immigrant in search of a locale for a bank. There Herman met Elizabeth Davis, who had come there with her parents from Liverpool, England. Upon their arrival in United States at New Orleans, the Davises boarded a steamboat and went up the Mississippi and Missouri rivers searching for a place to settle. The broad vista of land across from Council Bluffs, Iowa, looked appealing, so the family settled there. Soon thereafter Kountze and Davis married and prospered, while also becoming the parents of a large family, including daughter Eugenie.[24]

In September 1895 Nicholson announced his engagement to Eugenie to the Judah family in a typically mock-heroic indirect way: "My dear Friends: I am able to say now to you who have been so kind to me that it is all satisfactorily arranged at last, and my engagement to Miss Kountze may now be known not only where the Kaw and the Platte roll seaward, and among the pines and hills of Maine, but where the sunlight falls on the placid waters

MEREDITH NICHOLSON III

Eugenia and Meredith Nicholson.

of Maxinkuckee." Nicholson concluded, "She will be here shortly, when I hope you will all see her."[25]

The couple planned an April wedding, but, as Nicholson informed the Judahs "on the day that was to have been my wedding, but is not," Eugenie was not in Omaha, but instead was in Florida looking after her brother, recently married himself but seriously ill with typhoid fever. Nicholson closed this letter, written in Indianapolis because of the wedding's postponement, with a listing of his current reading (three novels) and a comment on how wonderful life was in Indiana:

> not a bad place to be—this. The spring is very sweet here in Indiana. There are tranquil twilights, and calm mornings when one who cannot wheel is prone to walk to town down Meridian street's long vista. And on side streets, wher [*sic*] of course no polite people are found, there are lilac bushes that make one give a happy gasp. Isn't Whitman responsible for "When lilacs last in our dooryard bloomed?"—and I am sure it is my friend Charles Warren Stoddard who has said "lilacs, purple lilacs in full bloom", and again he calls the "cool purple liacs" [*sic*]. Yes, it is Indiana—at this time, and again in October.[26]

As their second choice, the couple decided upon a June wedding. At a large church wedding in Omaha on June 16, 1896, the couple married. Tarkington, still an unpublished novelist, was Nicholson's best man.[27] Nicholson, however, assured the Judahs he would rather have them "at my wedding than any people I know, not excepting the Czar, Signor Crispi, and King Menelek [*sic*]." By then, too, Nicholson was already planning "to try my hand at a story after I have whipped [another] book of verses into shape," but first there was the necessity of providing a living for himself and his wife (or at least giving the appearance of doing so).[28]

4

And They Lived Happily Ever After

"Everywhere the increase of divorce is appalling. The subject is constantly discussed in all its connotations. The American home, we find, is not the unassailable fortress of happiness and loyalty it was fifty, or even twenty-five years ago."[1]

MEREDITH NICHOLSON, 1925

THE TITLE OF ONE OF NICHOLSON'S LAST NOVELS, AN ATTEMPT at realism rather than romance, can apply to his own life with two caveats. First, his blissful and productive married life did not begin at once. There was a difficult interlude in which he tried—unsuccessfully—to become, like his father-in-law, a businessman, and his career and marriage blossomed only when, at his wife's urging and support, he became a full-time writer. Second, the happy partnership between Meredith and Eugenie Kountze Nicholson ended in 1931, upon Eugenie's death. Otherwise, the marriage transformed Nicholson's life and opened doors to him that would have been forever closed. For a long time indeed, "they lived happily," but not "ever after."

When the Nicholsons came to Indianapolis, evidently following a short honeymoon trip to the East, they showed up at the old homestead at 1033 North Capitol Avenue and began married life living with Nicholson's mother.

From this location on the near north side of downtown Indianapolis, Nicholson returned for only a short time to the *Indianapolis News*. Soon, in keeping with Herman Kountze's wishes and example, Nicholson tried his hand in business. The first venture was as a stockbroker, an unusual choice for someone who never liked numbers, but he took the work seriously and tried hard. He did, however, also keep up an interest in poetry. His regular poetic contributions to the local press are one indication of this continuing passion; another is the comment of a friend, George C. Calvert, after a leisurely visit to the brokerage office in July 1898. "Yesterday," said Calvert, "I loafed a long time with Meredith Nicholson. He is truly a delightful fellow, —as he would say, a 'bully fellow,' and he has high ideals for his poetry, too. I think we are destined to read more of his verse that really attains to the true dignity of poetry. Since he has gotten away from the work of the newspaper office, he is writing less and writing what he does more carefully and with more artistic finish and detail."[2]

Limited success in the first business venture caused Nicholson to begin looking elsewhere for both employment and time to write. He first applied for editing positions in the East, probably without much hope of finding one. He sent feelers out to the *Washington Post*, where his first editor at the *Sentinel*, Scott C. Bone, served as managing editor, and to papers in New York City and Boston, but there were no takers. Soon, with the help of his father-in-law, Nicholson headed west rather than east, and became an officer in one of the Kountze-controlled businesses in Colorado.[3] Again, in a surprising choice of occupations, Nicholson agreed to become the treasurer and auditor of a mining company in Denver, where Charles H. Kountze, Eugenie's uncle, was a banker. It also seems that the Kountze brothers were the majority owners of the Northern Coal Company that employed Nicholson.

The Nicholsons moved to Denver in the fall of 1898, taking up residence in a fine old house located at 1410 High Street, for which they paid $22,000. Evidently, the Kountzes, or perhaps just Eugenie, helped in its purchase, but now Nicholson was well established in his adopted city. Again he tried hard to be a successful businessman, and he was, but the work was not satisfying and he was appalled at some of the shady business practices he observed from his vantage point inside the company.

In other ways, however, the Denver years were pleasant and memorable ones for Nicholson. By happy coincidence, the Reverend Myron Reed had gone to Denver following his years in Indianapolis, and Nicholson for a short while was able to continue hearing the sermons of one of the heroes of his youth. To Nicholson, Reed was "one of the most interesting and original thinkers Indianapolis has known," and Reed became Denver's "most popular preacher" before his death in 1899. The Nicholsons also became parents of two daughters during this time. Elizabeth was born in March 1899, and Eugenie, named for her mother, came along in the fall of 1900. Tragically, however, this child was sickly and died in January 1901. The Nicholsons' other two children, Meredith Jr. (born 1902) and Charles Lionel (born 1906), came after their parents had returned to Indianapolis.[4]

The dispiriting work in the coal business and the excitement, as well as the toils and troubles, of parenthood were eventually overcome by a remarkable writing opportunity that came Nicholson's way in 1899. For someone with only an eighth-grade education and no works of prose beyond his newspaper articles, the invitation to write a book about Indiana was astonishing. Nevertheless, building upon their chance meeting in Cambridge soon after Nicholson's first book of poetry had appeared, Professor George Edward Woodberry of Columbia University decided to give the Denver businessman and erstwhile poet this opportunity.

Woodberry, who served as the general editor for a series of National Studies in American Letters, invited Nicholson to prepare a volume on Indiana's literary achievements. Nicholson's well-received slim volume of verses, *Short Flights* (1891), had earned Woodberry's respect, and perhaps Nicholson also had been recommended to him by librarians at the public library and the state library in Indianapolis, who certainly remembered the young man as a frequent visitor and a talented, ambitious writer.

However it happened, Nicholson's selection turned out to be an inspired choice. In only a year, he penned a remarkably full and detailed study of Indiana's literary, social, and political culture that went far beyond the initial plan for the series. Titled simply *The Hoosiers* (1900), this work, Nicholson's only history among his twenty-eight books, has become a minor classic within the historiography of the state. In Woodberry's view, the book was "an admirable one on a difficult subject," and he told Nicholson that he had "shown the qualities I hoped you would in handling it." Slightly revised and reprinted at the time of the state's centennial, *The Hoosiers* went through eight more printings in 1915 and 1916. This is all the more remarkable given the embryonic status of state history at the time of the book, there being only one history (by a journalist) of Indiana already in print, and it is not cited by Nicholson. There were, however, some helpful studies by professional historians of the state's territorial beginnings and of its role in the Revolutionary War, the scene of George Rogers Clark's brilliant campaign in the West, but nothing had yet been written on the state's literary culture.[5]

Nicholson also had the difficulty of distance to overcome, for his preparation of the book required much work in libraries within Indiana, as well as in the Denver Public Library. In his short preface dated "Denver, July, 1900," Nicholson acknowledged the assistance of a few other writers, including Edward Eggleston, Anna Nicholas, Merrill Moores, and May Louise Shipp. The latter, a close friend of both Meredith and Eugenie Nicholson, had provided the author with the very helpful papers of "her kinswoman," Julia Dumont (1794–1857), identified in the book as "the first Hoosier to become known beyond the State through imaginative writing" and "among all the light-bringers of the first half of the century," as "one of the most distinguished." She was one of Eggleston's teachers in Vevay, Indiana. Nicholson also acknowledged the assistance of librarians in Indianapolis, Crawfordsville (at Wabash College), and Denver.[6]

The Hoosiers opened with a chapter, twice reprinted since in major anthologies, on "Indiana and Her People." Here, in what he referred to in the preface as a "slight review of Indiana's political and social history," Nicholson developed themes that since have been recognized by Indiana historians as the ones most important to an understanding of the state's early development. He then moved on to identify major towns on the Indiana frontier, many of which have since lost their prestige, and to name a number of pioneer Hoosiers whose achievements brought fame to themselves and to their state. The list is long and contains a few surprises, but it included most of those subsequently recognized as influential leaders in politics, the law, and the arts. Nicholson also used imaginative works, primarily from the pens of Eggleston and James Whitcomb Riley, whose novels and poems provided source materials. For example, Nicholson borrowed Eggleston's description of a Whitewater River valley town in 1840:

> The stumps stood in the streets; the mud was only navigable to a man on a tall horse; the buildings were ugly and unpainted, the people were raw immigrants dressed in butternut jeans, and . . . the taverns were new wooden buildings with swinging signs that creaked in the wind.

While admitting that "old residents" considered this description unfair, just as they disliked Eggleston's descriptions of Hoosiers generally in his famous novel, *The Hoosier Schoolmaster* (1871), Nicholson said that life in troubled conditions on the frontier nevertheless produced families "associated with the best that was thought and done in the community." His examples of outstanding pre-Civil War Hoosiers included Henry Ward Beecher, pastor of the Second Presbyterian Church in Indianapolis from 1839 to 1847, and the members of the Indianapolis Literary Club, established in 1877.[7]

Nicholson also managed to toss in a bit of humor with his remark that Indiana was a state "where not to be an author is to be distinguished." George Ade (and others) later expanded upon this point of Indiana's widespread interest in writing through a story about a lecturer who invited authors in the audience to join him on the stage, and everyone came forward! Nicholson closed his introductory chapter with yet another reference to the seemingly universal habit of versifying among Hoosiers by mentioning how a retired banker, "who had never been suspected, began to inveigle friends into his office on the pretext of business, but really to read them his own verses." "Rhyming is," Nicholson opined, "the least harmful of amusements," without mentioning his own proclivities here.[8]

The second part of Nicholson's book opened with the perennial question all Indiana people confront: the origins of the word "Hoosier" and how it became affixed to people in Indiana. Nicholson first offered many of the now standard explanations, and credited John Finley's early poem "The Hoosier's Nest" (1830) with having helped attach the word to residents of Indiana, but in the end, as is still the case, he could come to no definitive answer. Instead, in the balance of the second chapter, Nicholson took up the question of a distinctive Hoosier dialect and revealed his wide-ranging reading in a variety of memoirs, novels, and poems, even songs, for his samples. His surprising, even daring conclusion was that there really was no such thing. "The so-called Hoosier dialect," he suggested, "where it survives at all, is the speech of the first American settlers in Indiana, greatly modified by time and schooling, but retaining . . . the peculiarities that were carried westward from tide water early in the nineteenth century." Moreover, the speech of the Indiana pioneers contained "comparatively few words that are peculiar to the State or to communities within it." Nicholson expected a tide of criticism from his reviewers and the reading public regarding this point, and he was prepared to defend it with even more examples, but he had made the point well and persuasively, and no challenges emerged.[9]

After the opening general chapters, Nicholson moved easily into more specific discussions of "Bringers of the Light," his term for the early preachers and teachers in the state; the "experiment in socialism" at New Harmony, which he visited in order to gather information on Robert and Robert Dale Owen, William Maclure, and Thomas Say; and two major "interpreters" of Hoosiers, Eggleston and Riley. He must have had great fun, and great pride, in writing the chapter about the "Hoosier Athens," a term that referred to his beloved Crawfordsville, home to Wabash College and many significant writers, only four of whom Nicholson profiled—Lew Wallace, Maurice Thompson, and the Krout sisters, Mary and Caroline. His study of other Hoosier writers, in a chapter he called "Of Making Many Books There Is No End," gave attention to other novelists as well as to historians and politicians who had contributed to Indiana's literary productivity through memoirs and reminiscences. The final chapter, named with a uniquely Nicholson touch "An Indiana Choir," discussed Hoosier poets, particularly the little known but worthy couple, Forsythe and Elizabeth Conwell Willson, and their many "songs" about the Hoosier state.[10]

Remarkably elegant and graceful in its unhurried style (although we now know about the pressures of time and distance under which it was written), the book is also extraordinary in its comprehensive but restrained approach. Nicholson avoided obvious boastfulness and overreaching claims about his state's achievements, and he also modestly avoided even naming himself as one who was also a contributor to the sizable portfolio of writings by Indiana people. This holds true for the "Centennial Postscript" chapter he added for the book's second edition, which came out long after he had achieved repeated best-seller status with many novels.

The Hoosiers, a labor of love for its author, appeared in December 1900 and received good reviews. This would be expected, perhaps, from the Indianapolis press, but even Martin W. Sampson, the reviewer for *Dial Magazine*, concurred, calling the book "an excellent piece of work." Sampson also referred to the divergent opinions about Indiana's literary reputation. Most outsiders, he said, considered it "not enviable," whereas Hoosiers (as they call themselves, Sampson noted, but did not like others to do so) rather ruefully resented this attitude and "emphasized unduly the importance of what the state has already achieved." But Nicholson, he concluded, "did not fall into either camp and instead had "soberly essayed a *cultur-geschichte*," a true cultural history of Indiana.[11]

It is noteworthy, too, that many of the writers discussed in the book were known to Nicholson personally, quite an accomplishment for the unschooled boy who had grown up on the flats of White River. But these acquaintanceships had a downside, too. As Nicholson "whispered" to May Shipp, who had complimented Nicholson upon his work, "it is much easier to write of people who are safely dead that about those we are likely to meet around the next corner." Particularly this was true concerning Riley, who was "very sensitive" and who "once or twice fell out with me because in my newspaper days, I withheld the fullest praise from him in writing of his books." It was different for the more elderly Wallace and Eggleston, however, for Nicholson assumed that both had "practically closed their portfolios" by the time of the book. But Riley and many others were still actively adding to the list of their publications.[12]

The neophyte historian must have been especially pleased with the anonymous review of his book in the *Indianapolis Journal* that praised the book for its effort in analyzing "the hitherto neglected branch" of state history— "the development of literature" in Indiana. The reviewer also commended Nicholson for his insights regarding the state's early social and political development, "plainly the result of careful reading and investigation." The section on

Riley drew particular applause as the best "understanding" of the man and his work in print: "It is at once fair and sympathetic and admirable in tone." Overall, the reviewer lauded the book's "grace of style, its lightness of touch[,] and the deft weaving in of anecdote and illustration." The Woodberry-edited series on American letters had already attracted "unusual attention," and the reviewer predicted that *The Hoosiers*, the third book of the series, would receive "an equal welcome."[13]

A later article in the same newspaper supplied much more information on the author himself, after regretting initially that the author's modesty prevented him from including himself as one of the state's literary treasures. It then quoted at length from a story in the *Denver News* on "Mr. Nicholson's personality." The Colorado reporter first commented on the rarity of having "one of its clever business men [turn] his leisure into books of a quality that can be read and reread." He then quoted Nicholson to the effect that the "best thing" about him was "his wife and two babies" and that he shied away from saying "too much about himself." Concerning Eugenie Nicholson, the reporter referred to her "charming personality" and her "keen literary sense which makes her an ideal wife for a literary man."[14]

Nicholson was described "as a newspaper man, one of the best types of journalists. He has the literary instinct to express his thoughts in clear, terse and polished English,

MEREDITH NICHOLSON III

Nicholson said he wanted his books "to prove that Indiana was not the country that God forgot."

which he loves with the appreciation of a true litterateur."
Physically, Nicholson was described as "rather above the
middle height and is broad-shouldered, but not rugged.
His face is pale and he looks at you with a shrewd pair
of rather small, gray eyes which have the faculty of being

inscrutable if he wills it that way. He could be as stolid as a graven image—or he can 'let himself go' and the appreciative face of a man of letters is there."[15]

The *Indianapolis News* reviewer was also favorably impressed by *The Hoosiers* and summarized large portions of it, saying it "will be read with pleasure" not only by Hoosiers but all those interested in the region of which Indiana is a part. Critical only regarding Nicholson's generous inclusion of some writers perhaps not worthy of mention and of Nicholson's omission of himself, who has written "many poems" of great beauty, "the best of which have a spiritual power which has not often been excelled" by any other Hoosier, the reviewer concluded by calling *The Hoosiers* "a loving tribute from a man in love with his theme. Justice, measure, absence of exaggeration, and good sense are its most marked traits. It is well written and is clearly the product of much reading and careful study."[16]

In almost a postpartum mood of exultation and exhaustion following the publication of his first prose work, Nicholson visited Indianapolis in early December, sat for a lengthy interview with a reporter from the *Indianapolis News*, and then departed for a weeks-long recuperative visit to Point Comfort, Virginia. He blamed "continuous work in the high altitude of Denver" for his health problems and emphasized that he was "still a Hoosier . . . born in the low, flat lands, and have not yet become accustomed to living so far above the sea level."[17]

In discussing the book, Nicholson took great pride in having the Indiana volume as the third one in the Macmillan series, the two prior volumes being on Cambridge and Brook Farm, Massachusetts. "It is highly complimentary [to the state]," he asserted, "to come third in such a series."[18]

"There is no reason," he added, "why Crawfordsville, which by the way is my hometown, should not be as famous as Cambridge, though Wabash College can not, as it appears, play football much better than Harvard," and he believed that Caleb Mills, of Wabash College and the man to whom Nicholson dedicated the book, "was unquestionably one of the most useful of Indiana's educators." Continuing, Nicholson said that the chapter on Hoosier dialect, still an untouched subject academically, gave him the greatest difficulty, and he praised the initial work by Indiana's premier historians at the time, particularly John P. Dillon and Jacob Piatt Dunn Jr. In responding to a question about the book's small size, Nicholson said he had had great difficulty in collecting the materials for his research, but in the end he had "a very complete library of books relating to Indiana, as well as the writings of Indiana authors. I wrote many letters in collecting data, as books of reference, as usual, did not contain many of the names I have brought together."[19]

The Nicholsons returned to Denver via Saint Louis, where they happened to bump into Riley shortly before his performance that evening in the "big Odeon" Theater. With tickets provided by Riley, they were able to see the "entertainment" as "he played upon the emotions of several thousand people with an ease that made us proud to see." Sadly, however, their memorable evening in Missouri was the prelude to a difficult winter in Colorado, and Nicholson's euphoria over the warm reception given to his essay in historical writing would soon disappear.

In Denver "sickness" was everywhere, even among the doctors and nurses, and both Nicholson girls became ill. Unfortunately, the younger one, Eugenie, just under four months old, died on January 26, 1901. Soon afterwards, the Nicholsons decided to leave Denver—"say farewell to the mountains for all time," in Nicholson's words—and go eastward, somewhere. They considered several destinations, with Nicholson looking into the possibility of returning to newspaper work while also planning to concentrate more on his literary life. His exasperation with work at the mining office comes through in a letter (one of the few from this period that has survived) to his wife, who had gone with daughter Elizabeth (Bettie), to stay for a time with her parents in Omaha. "I was busy with cypher [*sic*] messages [telegrams] at Barbee's office when your message came," he explained. "We get instructions hourly and before we can act on them they are countermanded." For example, three times Nicholson was told to "stop all negotiations" with Barbee, but the next day he was ordered to "renew negotiations." He continued, "I called a meeting and we all roasted the K. Bros. [probably this refers to the Kountze brothers] for a lot of wobbly wobbles who don't know their own minds two minutes ahead—the wild telegraphing goes on."[20]

By then, too, Nicholson was looking into an intriguing newspaper co-ownership possibility in Indianapolis. Believing that the *Indianapolis Journal* would be sold, Nicholson tried to become one of the buyers, but, as he told his wife, "Williams was firm that one-sixth would not do." And, he added, "I'm really not sorry." He believed that another of the partners was to be Senator Charles Warren Fairbanks, a candidate for the presidency who would naturally want a newspaper to tout his effort. Nicholson definitely did not want to run such an operation. "Besides," he said, "[it] would interfere with our own family life if I had to spend my evenings at the office." Moreover, he proclaimed, perhaps to himself as much as to his wife, "I am now back at the place where I want to take my year off, and *try* to write." If an "opening" developed in Indianapolis, he said, "I should favor going [there] so as to have some background of support." If not, he was "a good deal disposed" to stay in the East, get a furnished house, and remain there for at least a year. The advantage, however, of going to Indianapolis was "that we have friends there" and "some good business opportunities might offer," whereas "such things can not be managed from a distance."[21]

Nicholson had stayed in Denver overseeing some house repairs and the sale of the house and was frustrated at being away from his wife and family for long periods, but in his solitude he continued writing, even as he missed Eugenie's assistance and support in those matters. He reported to his wife that, while working on "an address," daughter Bettie's "smiling little face is looking right at me as I write," and she looks "so much like her 'mudder.'" Later, in another of his frequent notes to Eugenie, he admitted to being "mighty lonely here" and stated that he was "heartily tired of this life I am leading."[22] Nonetheless, he continued to write (speeches, poetry, and perhaps even the early pages of a novel). In fact, on the day of his departure from Denver, June 10, 1901, Nicholson was too busy to visit the cemetery and his daughter's grave as planned, but he sent Eugenie a "carbon" of a forthcoming speech to be delivered in Indianapolis, asking for her suggestions. "Wire me," he said, "if you dislike any of it at the University Club [in Indianapolis]." He then caught a 10 p.m. train heading eastward towards the Hoosier State, where Eugenie soon joined him.[23]

Several weeks later, alone again and living in the University Club, he told his "dearest Genie" that he had been "a busy young thing since you left, first with house matters and then with lit'ry matters." The former included arrangements for the construction of a new house on fashionable North Delaware Street; the latter included a rhyme he had "fretted out" regarding the death of President William McKinley. "Between ourselves," he confided, "I think it pretty bad, and if you were here I'd probably not be suffered to print it." He also "dumped" some items, including "two little 7 & 4 line things, apropos of the president" into the *News* office. Fellow writer and reporter Anna Nicholas, at the *Journal*, had requested something for her newspaper too, but "I'd better cultivate the *News*, I think." Obviously Nicholson had no intention of returning to a morning newspaper, but he held out the possibility of joining the staff of an evening paper, as he started out on his self-granted, perhaps Kountze-funded, "sabbatical."[24]

5

The Main Chance

*"It is not enough to say that Warry Raridan could lead a german
or tie an Ascot tie better than any other man on the Missouri River;
for he was also the best informed man in that same strenuous valley
concerning the traditions of the English stage, and was a fairly good
actor himself, as amateurs go. He had an almost fatal cleverness,
which made him impatient of the restraints of college; and he left
in his sophomore year owing to difficulties with the mathematical
requirements. Good books had abounded in his father's house, and he
was from boyhood a persistent, though erratic reader. . . . He had a
slight literary gift, which he cultivated for his own amusement."*[1]

MEREDITH NICHOLSON, 1903

THE TITLE OF MEREDITH NICHOLSON'S FIRST NOVEL, PUBLISHED
in 1903, serves here as a metaphor for the sea change in
the author's life, as he decided to become, if possible, a
full-time writer while also providing for himself and his
family. It is perhaps a little odd, given his depth of knowledge about the Hoosier State and his belief, acquired in
part from James Whitcomb Riley, that one should write
about what one knows best, that this first book was set
in Omaha, Nebraska, not in Indiana. But Nicholson also
knew Omaha fairly well, was a quick study (as his efforts
with *The Hoosiers* had shown), and the book used a business theme, which he also knew well.

In order for Nicholson to take his own "main chance" at drastically changing his life, however, he had first to make satisfactory living arrangements in Indianapolis. The long-range plan involved building a house for the Nicholson family, then consisting of three members and soon, with the births of Meredith Jr. (1902) and Charles Lionel (1906), to grow to five, but in the short term the Nicholsons found housing for the family in an older home at 1322 North New Jersey Street. There, according to family legend as recorded by Allegra Stewart, Eugenie Nicholson converted one of the bedrooms into a study for her husband and said triumphantly as she displayed her handiwork to the would-be writer, "Now, write!"[2]

This was an invitation or an order Nicholson readily responded to, for he continued his literary activities with great gusto. Book reviews, poems, tributes to and obituaries for others, and a few public appearances for talks and readings soon followed. He even made the first of dozens of appearances in the prestigious *Atlantic Monthly* (October 1902) with his short poem "Wide Margins," soon followed by an invited biographical sketch of Edward Eggleston, about whom he had also written at length in *The Hoosiers*. Eggleston, a native Hoosier, had switched from being a Methodist preacher and a journalist to the writing of novels in the 1870s, his most important works being *The Hoosier Schoolmaster* (1871), *The Circuit Rider* (1874), and *Roxy* (1878). Subsequently, he turned to history and wrote a two-volume study of life in the United States, which led to his selection as president of the American Historical Association in 1900. Nicholson admired the work of both Edward and his younger brother, George Cary Eggleston, and contributed a overview of the life and works of the former. He surveyed Eggleston's entire body of work; pronounced balanced judgments on the novels, not great literature but "homely stories of the early Hoosiers" that will also "teach as history"; and noted that the author was also a "natural etymologist," a true scholar, and that he had "earned for himself a place of honor in American letters."[3]

Shortly after returning to Indianapolis in 1901, Nicholson was invited to join on stage the best-known and celebrated Indiana authors from all parts of the state in order to raise money for a proposed Benjamin Harrison monument. U.S. Senator Charles W. Fairbanks presided over the two-night entertainment held on May 30 and 31, 1902, a "literary feast," he boasted, "that can be prepared nowhere else than in Indiana."[4]

Evidence supporting this statement, probably considered hyperbolic even by Hoosiers, comes not only from general awareness of the talents and multiple publications of Indiana writers such as George Barr McCutcheon, Charles Major, Lew Wallace, Maurice Thompson, and the incomparable Riley, but also from an article, reprinted in part in the *Indianapolis News*, by Frank Basil Tracy, an incredulous *Boston Transcript* reporter. Tracy discussed the "rise of the Hoosier" in business, statesmanship, and literature. According to him, Hoosiers were no longer objects of "ridicule and contempt," and the state over-all had become "an industrial beehive: cities have been builded as if by magic." Tracy noted that Indianapolis had "become one of the greatest railroad centers and con-vention cities of the country . . . and the character of its public men has greatly improved." He then cited several examples—Senators Albert J. Beveridge and Fairbanks; General Henry W. Lawton, "the great towering figure of the war in Spain"; and especially President Benjamin Har-rison. But, Tracy continued, "neither in industrial nor in political fields does Indiana's swift rise most astound us. It is by its literature that we are stricken dumb, for it is simply overwhelming us with its gifts." Tracy ended with references to nearly a dozen Hoosier writers, several of whom were best-selling novelists, but some of whom also wrote historical accounts or newspaper articles, such as former Secretary of State John W. Foster, whose history of American diplomacy was as "fascinating as any novel," and George Ade, "whose Modern Fables convulse the Sunday newspaper reader, even though the critics rage."[5]

In a similar vein, Ade himself remarked, upon com-ing to Indianapolis for his role in the Harrison monument benefit after an absence of several years, that the city was "a marvel to me," that it had undergone a "wonderful" transformation, and had become "a great and busy city and a beautiful city." Specifically, he thought "the changes about the Circle are most amazing. I went to the top of it this morning and saw the city below me spread out as a beautiful picture."[6]

The cream of the crop of Indiana authors assembled in Indianapolis at the English Theater to raise money for a cause that, despite their personal political affiliations, all supported. Harrison was Indiana's only resident of the

IHS, BASS PHOTO COMPANY COLLECTION, P130

Benjamin Harrison won election as the country's twenty-third president in 1888.

White House, having lived at his North Delaware Street home in Indianapolis both before and after his time in office. Born in Ohio and the grandson of former President William Henry Harrison, who also had Indiana ties but later resided in Ohio, Benjamin Harrison had come to Indianapolis in 1854 following his graduation from Miami (Ohio) University and the study of law for two years in Cincinnati, and he filled a number of public offices for his adopted city, state, and nation during a career that ended in 1901.[7]

With too many authors to speak in one evening, the event was held on consecutive nights, with the writers to speak on the second night filling a box reserved for them and the master of ceremonies, Senator Fairbanks. On the second night the opening night readers sat there with the senator. Otherwise, the house was packed, some of the audience even sitting in the fifty or sixty chairs placed in the orchestra pit. Nicholson, one of the second-night readers, was teamed with Wallace, Major, McCutcheon, Ade, Booth Tarkington, Evaleen Stein, and Mary H. Catherwood. All of these speakers (except Tarkington, a late arrival) had signed an open letter, addressed to Riley, asking that he read on the second night, too. All had, they admitted, accepted their invitations to speak upon the understanding that they would have "the pleasure and honor of appearing on the same platform with you." Riley was visibly moved by this appeal and readily consented, reading both "The Old Man and Jim," his poignant tale of Jim's ill-fated role in the Civil War that ended with the father's final farewell to him, "Well, good-by, Jim, take keer of yourse'f," and another audience favorite, "Out to Old Aunt Mary's."[8]

Nicholson, for his part in the program, read, among other pieces, his touching lament, "Watching the World Go By," first published in 1890. This poem, evoking the sadness a distant onlooker might feel as a "train of cars darts swiftly through the night" and then disappears, "an echo on the air," indifferent to the grieving "many souls that watch the world go by," had deeply moved a Kansas farmer's wife, who wrote the author upon first reading this work that it was a "correct picture" of her own life. The newspaper report about the Hoosier authors' get-together included a caricature of a round-faced Nicholson, dressed in black with a black hat jauntily perched on his head and a quill pen behind his right ear, carrying a scroll bearing the words "Watching the World Go By—Nicholson." Only Tarkington and Wallace were similarly honored with drawings.[9]

Immediately after setting up shop at home, Nicholson worked steadily on his first novel. Every day, he anchored himself in his new home office and labored on his story. Even on evenings that were free from social engagements, he stayed at the task, but no one, except for a few very close friends in Indianapolis and in the East, was aware of this endeavor. In November 1902, just over a year after he had begun, Nicholson sent the long manuscript of *The Main Chance*, by a "Mr. Wheeler," to the Bobbs-Merrill Company for publication consideration. Only Nicholson's friend, Hewitt H. Howland, an editor at the publishing house, knew that the mysterious Wheeler was Meredith Nicholson, and the several in-house readers who assessed the manuscript liked it enormously and predicted an outstanding literary career for "Mr. Wheeler." The cover was soon blown, of course, and upon publication of the book in May 1902 Nicholson took his place as another in a long line of successful Indiana novelists.[10]

The book, heavily promoted and frequently reprinted to keep up with demand, was a hit with the reading public. Although slow-paced and peopled, for the most part, with ordinary folk from familiar walks of life, *The Main Chance* was expertly plotted and built to a surprising, but happy, conclusion. The characters were deftly drawn, particularly those of the lithesome banker's daughter and the Yale-educated former rancher who had come to the western city of "Clarkson," like Omaha, on the Missouri River, to represent the interests of investors from the East. Nicholson also sprinkled a heavier dose of humor throughout the book than he did in later works. He used, for example, a line reminiscent of the famous insult to William Jennings Bryan, the "Boy Orator of the Platte [River]," which said the label was appropriate because the river was only "an

THE
MAIN CHANCE

By the Author of
"THE PORT OF
MISSING MEN"

By MEREDITH NICHOLSON

IHS

Cover to a reprint of Nicholson's book The Main Chance.

inch deep and a mile wide at the mouth." One of Nicholson's characters said his friend was like the Juniata River
(in Pennsylvania), which was "very beautiful and very shal-
low." He also had a main character, a lifelong and proud

resident of Clarkson (like Nicholson and Indianapolis) say to a visitor that there were "just as interesting things to see here in Clarkson as there are in Venice and Rome" and that it would "take him a month to show her half the sights."[11]

The heart of the story, perhaps a little daring because Nicholson's father-in-law was also an Omaha banker, concerned a Clarkson banker, with (like the real one) a beautiful and talented daughter, and his efforts to get control of the city's traction company. In fact, the opening line of the book has the banker, William Porter, telling a visitor, "Well, sir, they say I'm crooked." He later repeated the line, adding, "but they don't say it very loud!"[12] The story then delves into the lives of the people around Porter—his family, his employees (including one with a mysterious background), their friends, and the visitor from the East, John Saxton, who becomes the book's protagonist. Intrigue is supplied as a rival businessman quietly seeks to get control of the traction company, too. There is also a kidnapping episode involving the banker's son, based apparently upon the then-recent abduction of the young son of Edward A. Cudahy, the meatpacking scion of Omaha.

In terms of his character development and his true-to-life depiction of life and people in the West, according to a prerelease report, "Those who know say Nicholson has captured the setting perfectly, and that the sons and daughters of Omaha walk in his pages and talk in his sentences." Two days later a review in an Indianapolis newspaper artfully summarized the novel without giving away its ending, and said the book "as a whole, is a clean, clearcut and clever piece of work; it is marked throughout by fine felicity of phrase, by bright and strikingly clever analysis of natives and character. It holds the interest of the reader."[13]

A lengthy review in a second Indianapolis newspaper, the *Journal*, complete with a large photograph of the new novelist, was also highly favorable. The reviewer particularly liked Nicholson's diction, his use of realistic people and situations, and the novel's structure: "There are no superfluities, no pages that can be skipped. It is entertaining throughout." The critic concluded that in "this first novel . . . Mr. Nicholson has set a pace for Western writers. His book is at once an achievement and a promise—an admirable, well-rounded piece of literary [*sic*]; not a great novel, but a story well told and well worth reading, one that leaves the reader with the conviction that even better things may follow."[14]

To modern readers, however, there is a slightly jarring aspect to the novel through the overt racism of its characters, which was doubtlessly an accurate portrayal of attitudes at the time. Nicholson also makes countless references to the smoking habits of virtually all the male characters—pipes, cigars, cigarettes—evidently a habit that he himself had acquired and permitted within his family. In

Frontispiece drawing for The Main Chance.

fact, at one point, the bon vivant character, "Warry" Raridan, is reported to believe "that the smoking of a cigarette
gave a touch of elegance to a gentleman."[15] But none of
the female characters here (and few in his other novels)
were tobacco users in public.

Interestingly, too, the name of Warrick Raridan, one of the main characters in *The Main Chance*, was used for character names in Nicholson's very first prose piece, "Tale of a Postage Stamp," which was written nearly twenty years earlier. This piece, the work of an already skillful writer, showed many signs of Nicholson's talents as a novelist. The tale was about an animated stamp, thankful that it was a postage stamp and not a "vulgar revenue-stamp, fit only to adorn a box of ill-smelling cigars or grace a barrel of inferior liquor!" and told the story of the stamp's owner, Archibald Warrack, an artist, and his brief love affair with a young woman, Helen Rariden, who sailed abroad, did not write or return, and finally married an English lord. When another stamp, a blurry one—it had been used and "cancelled," hence the streaks across its visage—that shared the desk drawer with the narrator, gasped at the revelation of this romantic betrayal, "The devil!" Nicholson, through the stamp, wisely concluded, no, "'Not the devil, the way of the world,' said I."[16]

The Main Chance quickly moved onto the best-seller list for 1903 and remained there for quite some time. In November, six months after its appearance, the *Indianapolis Journal* seemed pleased to report that in both October and November, according to *Bookman* magazine, *The Main Chance* was one of the country's most popular books and, the *Journal* noted, it was the only "first novel by a new author" to make the list. The paper attributed its continu-

Cover to Nicholson's Zelda Dameron.

ing success to recent eastern sales, the book's setting in the West leading to earlier sales in that region.[17]

While pleased at the book's reception (and offers to adapt it to the stage), Nicholson did not let himself become distracted, as he was busy with both the final plans for his spectacular new home on fashionable North Delaware Street, constructed and furnished in 1903, and with writing a second novel. This book, published in 1904 (as Nicholson established the amazing pace, one that he maintained for most of his writing career, of issuing one new book a year), had Indianapolis as its setting. The title character in *Zelda Dameron* was someone who, like Nicholson, had returned home to the capital city after an extended absence. This device let Nicholson describe the city called "Mariona"—Indianapolis is in Marion County—and the substantial changes in its appearance and amenities during recent years. Many of the places described had real-life counterparts—the "Hamilton Club" was the Columbia Club; "High Street" and "Jefferson Street" were, respectively, Meridian and Washington streets, the two major thoroughfares of Indianapolis; Lockerbie Street, famed as the street on which Riley lived, appears as "Harrison Street"; and many recent events in the city's life, such as the repaving of various downtown streets and the introduction of the interurban, are mentioned as well, as was Indiana's "swing state" reputation in national elections—"its votes were 'never reliably' the asset of any party," yet its electoral votes had "long been essential" to the victorious candidate and party. Veteran newsmen and other longtime residents of the city delighted in discovering the veiled references to streets and clubs, people and places known to them.[18]

Again, capably plotted with an element of mystery concerning the true identity of Zelda's parents, the book was primarily a novel of manners, of life in the Midwest at the turn of the century. Oddly, perhaps, given the straitened circumstances of Nicholson's early life, the book is concerned with the city's upper classes (Nicholson's own new classification) just before the advent of the automobile.

Zelda Dameron, a popular romance that sold well but in numbers considerably below that of *The Main Chance*, had been submitted to the publishers shortly after the Nicholsons moved into their new home. As described in the newly founded *Indianapolis Star*, the house at 1500 North Delaware Street was an exquisite, thoroughly "livable home." It was a Georgian Revival structure that, from the exterior "was a faithful reproduction of the old colonial homes of Virginia, tiny window-panes, entrances, and all." Inside, some "colonial" features were maintained, such as a long, wide central hallway with large rooms at either side and a dining room at the end. But the color scheme was modern, and the interior furnishings were designed for comfort and gracious living, thanks largely to Eugenie's taste. But it was the library that brought the most praise. An upper-level room, this elegant study for the author was lined with "low built-in bookcases [that ran] all around the room," had a large, open red-brick fireplace, and was attractively and functionally furnished with a large desk and reading chair.[19]

Nicholson's Indianapolis home at 1500 North Delaware Street.
Today, the home serves as the headquarters of
the Indiana Humanities Council.

Perhaps some of the finishing touches to his second novel had been made while ensconced in his new study, but clearly Nicholson's top-selling, most popular book, *The House of a Thousand Candles* (1905), was the first one to be written in the new quarters, a fact that subsequently led to this residence becoming known as "The House of a Thousand Candles." The Nicholsons encouraged this designation by their practice, every Christmas season, of placing candles in the mansion's many windows.

6

The House of a Thousand Candles

"The lines of the walls receded as the light increased, and the rafftered ceiling drew away, luring the eyes upward. I rose with a smothered exclamation on my lips and stared about, snatching off my hat in reverence as the spirit of the place wove its spell about me. Everywhere there were books; they covered the walls to the ceiling, with only long French windows and an enormous fireplace breaking the line. Above the fireplace a massive dark oak chimney-breast further emphasized the grand scale of the room. From every conceivable place . . . innumerable candles blazed with dazzling brilliancy. I exclaimed in wonder and pleasure."[1]

MEREDITH NICHOLSON, 1905

AFTER BECOMING WELL KNOWN AS A NOVELIST, MEREDITH Nicholson was asked many times how he got his ideas for new stories and new plots. He freely admitted that he did not know, that he could not explain the process at all. He did attempt, however, in a brief analysis of the creative process for a local newspaper, to explain *when* new story lines usually came to him, and then he outlined his work habits. At first, Nicholson allowed that "the gods that pass out plots are fickle devils, and very whimsical in their bestowing of favors." He then stated, "preposterous though the thing be," that "my most novel ideas, and those that have been the most profitable when worked out, have come to me when I shaved!" Admitting that this "confession" might spark derogatory comments, such as "Why doesn't the man serve the cause of literature by cultivating whiskers?" or "His stuff tastes like lather," he nevertheless took the issue quite seriously and once consulted a distinguished psychologist in search of an explanation. The prompt answer, that "the mind in all departments is at its best in the morning hours immediately after sleep," was no help, Nicholson said, because "I always shave at 6 o'clock in the evening." Then he further admitted that "even if I knew how to pull ideas out of the void, I should not be unselfish enough to give away the secret."[2]

He did point out, however, that before beginning a story, he "must see the end of it, or something at least that corresponds to a third act. A first chapter and all the intermediate incidents are comparatively easy if you have a strong dramatic end to lead up to." He also stressed the fundamental importance of characterization "in real novels." Indeed, throughout his career, Nicholson gave a richness and fullness to the descriptions of the main characters, particularly the women, who populated his novels.

The composition process itself usually involved many drafts of a particular work. Nicholson always wrote out the first draft by hand, then had it typed. At that point, in editing the copy, he would "tear it to pieces, get another [typed] copy, and so on, for half a dozen times if needed." Of course, some essays, or chapters, came out well the first time and needed little revision, but Nicholson was rigor-

*Nicholson sits in the study of his North Delaware Street home,
circa 1907*

ous in getting things just right before sending them on to
a publisher, and afterwards, too. As he mentioned in an
author's questionnaire for a publisher, his pet "hate," in
addition to lies and cats, was "typos."[3]

If we do not know exactly how the idea for *The House of
a Thousand Candles* came to him, at least we know where
he found the right locale for its setting and what he tried to
do in this, his third novel and far and away his most successful one. At the time, the most popular genre in fiction was
the adventure/mystery story, set in exotic places or in the
far-distant past. Current favorites were books by Hoosier

authors George Barr McCutcheon and Charles Major, but
the leading novel of this type was Anthony Hope's *The Prisoner of Zenda* (1896).[4] Nicholson wanted to try his hand,
too, at this kind of swashbuckling, thrilling adventure, but
one that would be set in his own time and in his own state.
While mulling over this plan, he visited his friend and neighbor, Alfred F. Potts, at Potts's summer home in Culver, Indiana. The house, now referred to in Culver as "The House of
a Thousand Candles" because of its association with Nicholson's famous book, was on Lake Maxinkuckee, and from its
location the towers of the Culver Military Academy could
be seen across an arm of the lake.

As Nicholson explained years later in an open letter
to the alumni of Culver High School, the idea for a setting for his new novel "struck me on a visit to Lake Maxinkuckee. It was at a time when many stories were being
written about imaginary kingdoms in Europe." Nicholson wanted, he said, to do "the same sort of yarn with an
American setting" and without "kings and princesses." He
decided upon "weaving a romance about the lake. The
towers of the Academy wore a sufficiently medieval air;
and I used winter scenes to create the necessary isolation.
Of course I changed the Academy into a girls' school and
took other liberties with the landscape. Once started I
had a lot of fun in the writing." This was obvious to most
Hoosiers because, for example, he worked in the name
of the lake used as the novel's setting by naming the ship

that carried the book's hero, John Glenarm, back to the United States in 1901 the "Maxinkuckee," and he made fun of himself as algebraically challenged by commenting on the name Devereaux. The "x" is the lady's name, he remarked through Glenarm, suggested "the algebra of my vanishing youth." He also managed, perhaps as a counterbalance to Glenarm's prejudicial comments about his new home state before he arrived there, some paeans of praise to the state's natural beauty, its wonderful lakes, and even its salubrious climate, though he did notice the weather's unpredictability: "April in Indiana! She is an impudent tomboy who whistles at the window, points to the sunshine and, when you go hopefully forth, summons the clouds and pelts you with snow!"[5] Having composed the book rapidly between October 1903 and April 1904, a particularly cold and snowy winter in Indiana, Nicholson later said that much snow "naturally got into the tale!"[6]

In a "self-interview" published in New York nearer the time of the novel's first appearance, Nicholson said the story, once he got into it, practically wrote itself, just "followed the wind's will," and that he "never assumed any responsibility for the characters or incidents." "It was all news to me," he said, "and I shall never know again the same pleasure I experienced in running upstairs every evening to my workroom to see just what was going to happen next. The very name of the book was an inadvertence. It slipped from the pen without premeditation."[7]

Having hit upon a general locale—a northern Indiana lakeside—for his new story, Nicholson next needed a very specific setting, and he chose to make it a most distinctive house. Described at length in the novel as a large mansion, still incomplete, but with statuary; stained-glass windows; large, creaky doors; an enormous fireplace; and a library lined with bookcases, it also featured secret passageways, hidden vaults, and dungeonlike cells used for storage. This unusual structure was neither the one in Culver that Nicholson visited in 1904 nor the one in Indianapolis in which he lived. Instead, its physical appearance was similar to one Nicholson had seen and been impressed by in Denver. From this elegant late-nineteenth-century mansion, built in the 1890s by the Reverend Richard S. Sykes, minister of the First Universalist Church, Nicholson got the idea, too, of a cryptic message carved in the oak paneling above the fireplace mantel.

Told in the voice of Glenarm, the grandson of the eccentric John Marshall Glenarm, the tale revolves about the efforts of the young bachelor narrator to live up to the terms of his grandfather's will, so that he would inherit Glenarm House in Wabana County, Indiana. The terms included living in the house for a year while "demeaning himself meanwhile in an orderly and temperate manner."[8] If he failed to do so, the property, house, and grounds would go to a Miss Marian Devereaux of New York.

The vagabondish Glenarm, upon learning of his grandfather's death while traveling in Italy, returned home at once, learned the details of his conditional inheritance, and decided, reluctantly, to accept the challenge and go "out there to spend a year." Upon arriving at an apparently

Cover of Nicholson's The House of a Thousand Candles.

"abandoned and lonely Indiana farm," Glenarm discovered that the estate came with a servant, Thomas Bates, already in place, a person who becomes a key figure in the narrative.[9]

Overall, the story is a gripping one, complete with late-night rendezvous, mysterious sounds, unknown visitors to the cavernous house, mistaken identities, occasional shoot-outs, the reappearance of one thought long dead, and, of course, an attractive girl, mysterious and alluring, as well as a double agent, too. In fact, Nicholson once called his story simply a "fairy tale with pistols."[10] To some, however, the scene in which a college-trained engineer from the Massachusetts Institute of Technology has a gun fight in the bowels of the darkened house, and another in the main hall of the mansion that pits Glenarm and his friends against the county sheriff and his "deputies," is absurd. It should be noted, though, that in the same year in which the novel was set (1901), the author's cousin had been gunned down on the streets of Seattle, Washington, in a desperate fight with the suspected operator of the city's notorious "box-houses" (saloons with stages attached to them) in its Skid Road section. The victim, William Luff Meredith, was the son of Nicholson's much-admired uncle, William Morton Meredith, to whom Nicholson had dedicated an early book. At the time of his assassination, Meredith had recently resigned as police chief of the city but was still engaged in a longstanding feud with his assailant, so violent and risky actions were not foreign to the author's own family experience.[11]

In the novel, if not in real life, all turned out well. Nicholson treated his readers to a most surprising conclusion, as true identities and previous associations among Nicholson's various characters were revealed, and the book turned out to be a smashing success. Initially published by the Bobbs-Merrill Company of Indianapolis in December 1905, the book had to be reprinted often and has been made into plays and motion pictures and issued in translation in at least eight other languages, including, as Nicholson told a publisher friend in Boston, one in "German (honest)."[12] Moreover, advertisers frequently used variations on the title in promoting their own products. One proprietor, business unknown, called his place "The House of a Thousand Scandals."

When Nicholson's blockbuster novel appeared, even the critics liked what the *New York Times* called "a story bristling with adventure," and the general public loved it.[13] Nicholson's previous novels had both reached bestselling status—*The Main Chance* had sold approximately forty thousand copies and *Zelda Dameron* about half that, but sales for *The House of a Thousand Candles* quickly jumped into six figures and the book has remained in print, making Nicholson, if not wealthy in his own right, at least a major contributor to his family's fortune. Moreover, as early as May 1906, plans were afoot for the story to be

Olivia

Frontispiece to The House of a Thousand Candles.

dramatized as a vehicle for actress Lulu Glaser, who wanted to go on stage as Marian Devereaux. In time, too, the book was picked up by two motion picture companies and made into silent movies. Nicholson complained later, however, that this arrangement was made by William Bobbs without consultation with or compensation for the author, and he took steps, in his subsequent contracts with publishers, to cover his rights regarding possible motion pictures. After 1908 his publisher was no longer Bobbs-Merrill, with whom he had a falling out regarding what Nicholson considered inadequate promotion and advertising of his books. (Eventually, after dealing with three other publishing companies, Nicholson returned to Bobbs-Merrill for the publication of his final two books in 1928 and 1929.)

Nicholson was quite proud of the work and delighted in its continuing fame and appeal across the continent, but he had some misgivings, too. He knew such literature did not meet the standard of realism, the "faithful presentation of reality," as opposed to romantic fiction, as espoused by noted American author William Dean Howells, and he vowed to reform soon. We also know the inspiration for the distinctive hat—a red tam-o'-shanter—worn by the heroine. Again, Nicholson freely admitted that the idea for dressing his character in the red tam came to him just as he was beginning the chapter featuring the lady. From his study on North Delaware Street, he happened to see a neighborhood girl walking to school that day wearing such a hat. The young girl, about twelve at the time the novel was being written, was Josephine Sharpe, later Mrs. Charles Latham, and the Nicholsons came to know her well. According to Charles Latham Jr., Josephine's son, Eugenie Nicholson occasionally called the Sharpe house and told Josephine that "Meredith wants to dance," so off they went. Whether she wore her red tam on such outings is not known.[14]

Nicholson also kept busy writing other short pieces and joining in the many activities in Indianapolis. He was particularly active in helping manage the affairs of the Contemporary Club as well as the Drama Club. His minor writings at this time included part of a memorial booklet to General Lew Wallace. Nicholson wrote the section dealing with Wallace as a writer. Others wrote about him as a soldier, a diplomat, and a citizen.[15] Nicholson also wrote a delightful essay about his adopted hometown for the *Atlantic Monthly*,[16] a few short poems, and two pieces, in 1904 and 1905, for *The Phi Gamma Delta*, the national magazine of the college fraternity in which Nicholson held honorary membership. This affiliation had come about through his association with Wabash College, which he did not attend but visited regularly.

Nicholson's visit in August 1905 to other college campuses in Lexington, Virginia, home to both Washington and Lee University and the Virginia Military Institute, prompted a touching essay on the city and its wonders. Captivated by the beauty of the Shenandoah Valley in midsummer, Nicholson conveyed his appreciation of the village nestled in the foothills, its two academic institutions, and his respect for General Robert E. Lee, the Confederate leader who served the final years of his life as president of Washington College

(1865–70), later renamed Washington and Lee University. In paying tribute to Lee, he spoke of the "noble dignity and sublime peace" in the recumbent statue, in white marble, that rests in the "quiet, bare little chapel at Lexington," above the crypt with Lee's remains. "I do not envy," he added, "the man his composure who can stand beside that beautiful testimony to Lee without emotion."[17]

After publication of *The House of a Thousand Candles*, Nicholson, now financially secure by his own labors and already active in the public and cultural life of his city, branched out even more. He became deeply involved in Democratic politics, consenting from time to time to be a candidate for office (while hoping he would not win), and was even mentioned by the *Washington Star* in 1906 as a possible candidate for the vice presidency.[18] The Nicholsons also began to take more extensive family vacations to Maine and Massachusetts, but Cape Cod was a place Nicholson did not particularly care for, so thereafter the family made regular summer trips to northern Michigan. Indeed, at some point, they purchased a home on Mackinac Island, both as a summer retreat for the family, now numbering five, and a place where Nicholson could continue his writing in splendid isolation. The house, identified simply as "the red house, adjacent to the Grand Hotel" in family records, must have been the historic Newberry Cottage (1888), which "sits on one of the choicest locations, next to the Grand Hotel" on Mackinac Island.[19]

Another major change in Nicholson's life after the *Candles* success was the opportunity to travel abroad. In August 1906, immediately following a family outing to Kennebunkport, Maine, Nicholson stopped off in New York City as the others in the family returned to Indiana. Boarding the *Carmania* with two friends from Indiana, Bishop Joseph M. Francis and Bobbs-Merrill editor Hewitt H. Howland, the little group sailed for England and visits to London, Oxford, Cambridge, and various other literary centers and points of interest. Sadly, because of the unfortunate disappearance of most of Nicholson's correspondence and other papers collected by his first wife, almost the only information regarding this trip comes from two letters to his dear friend, "Doctor" James Whitcomb Riley. One of the letters announced the trip, while the other (from Cambridge) described a brief portion of it.

Nicholson, uncertain of his abilities as a sailor, said he hoped to get one meal down "before internal strifes tear me apart," and he warned Riley that "if you hear of terrible tidal waves you may know—about Wednesday night—that I am spouting like a whale." Nearly a month later, writing from Cambridge, "the great poet-breeding university," he said it was a "blessed relief to escape from great magnificent London," and that "our inn," the Cambridge Arms Hotel, was "a dream of ease and comfort, to say nothing of good food" and that it "realizes the fondest pictures of fiction. H. [Henry] James may not have been as grand a liar after all." Nicholson enthused that Cambridge was "like the pictures, just as Windsor Castle is, only better." Other highlights of the trip were viewing the "ancient wall at Chester (at night)," seeing the mummies in the British Museum, attending the Oxford-Cambridge boat race on the Thames River, and visiting "the poet Gray's room in the Varsity here." In closing, Nicholson said that their small party was "pulling together heartfully. The Bishop understands the British money system, Doctor Howland knows the history of the country, and I am taking in much and saying little."[20]

As much as he enjoyed his first trip abroad, an experience he gave to most of his heroic characters in the early novels, Nicholson did not let it or other pastimes divert him from his major activity—writing novels. Indeed, perhaps as an indication that he was abandoning poesy in order to concentrate on prose, he gathered some three score of his favorite verses, even including four from *Short Flights* (1891), and in 1906 published a second and final book of his poems, titled simply *Poems*.[21] Nicholson never wrote any more verses for publication, except for the one he did as a special favor (after much pleading) for friend and fellow Wabash College man, Indiana governor Thomas R. Marshall. The ode, "To the Battlefield of Antietam," was written in 1910 to assist in Marshall's dedication of an enormous Indiana marker on the Antietam battlefield.[22] Nicholson also wrote, apparently not for publication, although it appeared in the press anyway, a short poem that he sent to his friend, now Vice President Marshall, upon the occasion of his inauguration. Telegraphed to Washington just moments before the daylong festivities began, Nicholson's words, which were framed and soon adorned the vice president's room in the capitol, paid homage to the humor and comic wit of the Indiana's newest "number two man" in the government:

> Happy the man that scales the h[e]ights afar
>   Blest by Olympian dews,
> But happier he whose wagon and whose star
>   Follow the comic muse.
>
> May you, Oh Hoosier, wrapt in toga bright,
>   Never the guiding lose
> Of that angelic daughter of Delight
>   We name the comic muse.
>
> Philosophy alert to heed her call
>   Nothing can long refuse
> Wisdom, encamped by folly's flimsy wall
>   Winks at the comic muse.[23]

Poems received decent reviews but very few sales. Using a "proem [to] James Whitcomb Riley" as the book's introduction, however, must have pleased Riley, for he purchased seventy-five copies of the book to distribute to his friends. Nicholson joked about this making up most of the sales of an insignificant book, but his true feelings about the work, and Riley's gesture, came out in a warm letter to its dedicatee:

> My dear Doctor: I shall feel better if I say in ink, what I tried to say in audible words, that your kindness to my little book of verses has pleased me and touched me as no other kindness toward any writings of mine, in any quarter, ever did. Probably no friend of mine understands, as you do, how much of a man's heart and hope go into poems no matter what their quality . . . . I have no false ideas as to the values of my verse. Its wings are mighty weak; but your kind aid will help the poor little chap to make a friendly harbor here and there.[24]

Nicholson realized his major talent, and financial opportunities, lay in writing novels and essays, and he maintained a torrid pace as a novelist in the years ahead, producing two books in 1907 and then at least one in each of the next few years. He also was more in demand as a speaker. In January 1909 he advised an English composition class at Wabash College that, in order to improve "the directness and conciseness" of their writing, they should "read the King James version of the Bible studiously," and a few months later, he preached a lay sermon at the All Souls Unitarian Church, perhaps on the same subject. He also contributed a preface to a friend's book (Kin Hubbard's *Abe Martin of Brown County, Indiana* [1906 and 1907]), and his remarks to the annual gathering of the Indiana Society of Chicago in 1909 appeared in its yearbook. About this time, Nicholson's name first appeared in *Who's Who in America*. His biography and his growing list of publications were in every edition of this publication from the fifth edition (1908) through the twenty-fourth (1947).[25]

Nicholson's first post-*Candles* book, on a new theme, was *The Port of Missing Men*, which appeared in February 1907. The novel was a drama involving the Austrian throne that was ultimately played out in the foothills of Virginia, not far from Washington, D.C. Memorable characters and intriguing and implausible, but not impossible, actions helped produce a robust story. Nicholson admitted privately that he did not like the book very much, but he thought the poetry selections used throughout were quite good. The novelist had set a high standard for himself in his first adventure story, and his later efforts sometimes suffered in comparison.

Nicholson's next book, *Rosalind at Red Gate*, published in November 1907, was also set in Indiana at the Saint Agatha School on Lake Maxinkuckee and was a sequel of sorts to *The House of a Thousand Candles*. Some of the

Cover of Nicholson's Rosalind at Red Gate.

characters from *Candles*, mainly John Glenarm's vagabond Irish friend, Larry Donovan, who had relocated to
the Midwest, reappeared in this book, and the result was
another popular triumph. One reviewer called it the "best
American mystery story of the year," and opined that the

author would suffer "no loss of reputation here."[26] Indeed, the book was frequently reprinted here and abroad and it also captured the interest of film producers.

Nicholson's final Bobbs-Merrill book, for the time being, was 1908's *The Little Brown Jug at Kildare*, later republished in England as *The War of the Carolinas*. As always, the book was deftly plotted and filled with interesting characters, particularly the governors of both North and South Carolina, their daughters and their respective suitors, and, from the other side of the tracks, a band of notorious moonshiners who kept eluding capture by one state's police force or the other by moving across the state line at opportune times. Of course, all works out well in the end for everyone, except the moonshiners, and each governor soon had a new son-in-law. Labeled "an amusing book" that was both "wholesome in tone, full of excitement and some fun," one reviewer concluded by saying this work was "to the novel what the farce-comedy is to the drama."[27]

Nicholson recognized the validity of such comments and was increasingly unhappy with producing light novels of this type. Even though they were popular with the reading public and regularly appeared on best-seller lists, he wanted to become a more serious writer of realism, according to the teachings and example of the two men he most admired, Howells and Matthew Arnold of England. "I plan," he promised, mainly to himself, "to write a really good novel if I keep life and health."[28]

7

Confessions of a Best Seller

"Having, as I have confessed, deliberately tried my hand at romance merely to see whether I could swim the moat under a cloud of the enemy's arrows, and to gain experience in the mechanism of story-writing, I now declare (though with no illusion as to the importance of the statement) that I have hung my sword over the fireplace; that I shall not again thunder upon the tavern door at midnight . . . . It has been pleasant to follow the bright guidon of romance . . . . But I feel reasonably safe from temptation. Little that men do is, I hope, alien to me; and the life that surges round me . . . speak[s] with deep and thrilling eloquence; and he who would serve best the literature of his time and country will not ignore them."[1]

MEREDITH NICHOLSON, 1909

INDIANA'S REPUTATION AS THE HOME OF AN OUTSTANDING number of popular writers, authors whose works appeared regularly on the nation's best-seller lists, seemed overblown to a newcomer to the state. So John H. Moriarty, Purdue University's new librarian in 1946, decided to test it. He examined Alice Payne Hackett's book, *Fifty Years of Best Sellers, 1895–1945* and analyzed her findings according to the home states of the nation's most popular authors. He assigned ten points for the top best seller in each year, nine points for the second, and so on down to one point for tenth place, and then added up the scores for each state. Incredibly to him and many others, Moriarty's figures showed that Indiana finished a close second to New

York, a state with four times Indiana's population. For the years studied, New York authors amassed 218 points, Indiana 213; Pennsylvania was in distant third place with 125 points.[2]

Meredith Nicholson played a large part in giving his home state this literary distinction, although he was quite aware that the best-seller list did not coincide with a list of the "best books," but rather the most popular works, and he was actually embarrassed to be there so often. He was,

The four authors that brought glory to the Hoosier State during the golden age of Indiana literature in the late nineteenth and early twentieth centuries. In the back row are (left to right) James Whitcomb Riley and Nicholson, while in the front row are (left to right) George Ade and Booth Tarkington.

of course, pleased at his early success in producing well-received books. He said that "no one but my neighbor and my neighbor's wife" ever read his first book, "an essay in history," but that from 1903 to 1909 his titles "were included fifteen times in the 'Bookman' list of best-selling books," and he once topped the list for "three months successively." But, as Nicholson indicated in the essay whose title is used at the head of this chapter, the "best selling" label really had little significance. Some retailers, he believed, reported as a "best-seller" a book they had purchased in advance in large numbers, thereby creating a "false impression of its popularity."[3]

Nicholson made these statements in an anonymously published article in the *Atlantic Monthly* (1909), wherein after "confessing" to having written many "best-selling" adventure stories over the previous six years, he announced his intention to abandon "cloak and pistols" and to write instead more realistic tales "about the life that surges around me." His uneasiness about his lightweight books had been expressed as early as 1906, when he told New Englander Henry Beers that he was "ashamed" of being a best-selling writer; that he wanted "to do solider stuff soon." He said to a reporter in 1910, "I've written my last fanciful romance." Yet he noted with pride, obviously referring to his three top sellers, "I hear a jug rolling down the gulch, to join my candlebox in the port of missing men," and he later boasted (in 1915) that "I now have [published] fourteen books and one [more is] in press." Just twenty years ago, as a newspaper man, Nicholson hoped only "for a few rhymes" to go out.[4] He was not totally abandoning interesting, absorbing tales and stories, because, as he stated elsewhere, unrelieved, dreary realism like that produced by Theodore Dreiser served no good purpose.

Nicholson's authorship of the "Confessions" article became widely known when this essay was included in his first collection of writings, *The Provincial American and Other Papers* (1912). An excellent assemblage of writings mainly from the *Atlantic Monthly*, the largely autobiographical essays held together well despite having been composed over a ten-year period. Nicholson, an admitted provincial himself, extolled the virtues of small-town life and democratic ideas, and as exemplars of these values included extended passages on various Indiana writers and politicians, particularly Edward Eggleston. He also urged church attendance by "Smith," his ordinary man in the street, and "the tired business man," his term for the backbone members of society.[5]

In the meantime, Nicholson set about putting theory into practice, but he still had one card to play. After his amazing success with adventure stories, he wrote a "farewell" novel, a "farce-comedy" intended as a parody to his earlier works, but most reviewers and readers missed the point and "this book also has been a 'best-seller'!"[6] Presumably, this was Nicholson's sixth novel, *The Little Brown*

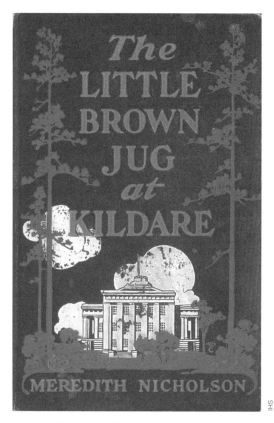

Cover to Nicholson's The Little Brown Jug at Kildare.

Jug at Kildare (1908), but, of course, to preserve at least the pretense of anonymity, the title of this book and the others did not appear in the article. Overall, however, the article and its autobiographical parts are sufficiently direct and clear so that, once Nicholson's authorship is known,

his comments and opinions about his first three novels can
be ascertained. And he did, as he pointed out to another
friend, try to do something entirely different in the first of
his post-"confession" books, *The Lords of High Decision*
(1909). When he ordered an advance copy of it for a "Mr.
Wicks," perhaps a reviewer, he said it was a "different sort
of book" and that "I hope there is a dash of moral health
in it. Be good to it."[7]

Nicholson amplified his thoughts about this book in
an article for *World's Work*, an essay that also appeared
in part in the *Indianapolis News*. In "What I Tried to Do
in My Latest Book," Nicholson said that the novel was
set in Pittsburgh, and that it explored "the manners and
morals of the ruling class amid the steel mills of the city."
The book got its dramatic force from the efforts of young
Wayne Craighill, a mill owner's dissolute son, to reform
himself and become worthy of the attentions of another
of Nicholson's more interesting female characters, the
beautiful, intelligent, and idealistic Jean Morley. Nicholson believed that his own experience of working for a coal
mining company in Denver, coupled with several months
spent looking at labor conditions in Pittsburgh, prepared
him sufficiently for good insights into his characters, the
conditions under which they lived, and the locale itself.[8]

In discussing his purpose in the "transition" novel,
Nicholson admitted his distaste for "problem or special-
plea novels" and suggested that "a great subject in itself

does not make a great novel; the characters must be clean-cut and authentic or they will express nothing. They must be human beings, made to exist, to suffer, and to grow before the reader's eyes." One can easily "describe" characters, but "the test of an author's quality lies in his ability to depict moral and spiritual change." Nicholson also admitted, "I am only about half realist; the romantic aspects of life—the lives that I see and touch—interest me immensely." Rather than a fiction that is either one thing or the other, Nicholson preferred "a 'blend' of the realistic and the romantic." To him, also, the Wayne Craighill character represented the city itself: "He gropes his way toward the light, much as the city itself is doing, he is . . . a man in search of his own soul; and, as he finds it through labor, so must the city, and one must be knowing in all its forms and expressions." Against the young Craighill, Nicholson "set up his father—the familiar, smug, complacent reformer, self deceived into believing that the rough edges of our difficult problems can be ground down smoothly by prayers and resolutions." Finally, however, he stated, "I can only hope that the story fulfills the first law of the novel, which is that it must entertain."[9]

In a long coda to his article, Nicholson praised the novels of others, such as American authors Winston Churchill and William Allen White, who so admirably addressed aspects of modern life, and he suggested, obviously with a tinge of sadness, that poetry was no longer "an adequate medium for those who would utter effectively the messages of democracy. Prose drama and the novel are far better adapted [for this purpose]."[10]

In other ways, too, Nicholson's life changed during the decade after he announced a new focus for his future novels. He did, despite the increasing demands upon his time by family and civic activities, keep up his remarkable productivity in books and articles, speeches, and a voluminous correspondence. At this time, too, he changed his publishers from Bobbs-Merrill to, for one book, Doubleday and Page, and then for seven more between 1910 and 1917, to the Houghton Mifflin Company in Boston. This in turn led to a delightful and extensive correspondence between Nicholson and two of the Houghton Mifflin editors, both authors themselves, who taunted and teased each other relentlessly. Nicholson's names for Ferris Greenslet and Roger L. Scaife (who later became the director of Harvard University Press) included Old Hoss, Old Sport, The Professor, and Porthos (in a letter signed by D'Artagnan). In the course of these years, the Nicholson children attended summer camp in New England, and their eldest daughter, Elizabeth, enrolled in an eastern finishing school, thereby giving the Nicholsons more reasons to travel to the Boston area and Meredith the chance to visit his new friends at Number 4 Park Street, the home office of the Houghton Mifflin Company. Nicholson even managed, through the courtesy of his new editors, to see his first football game (in the Yale Bowl) in October 1914. The next year he also managed, upon his daughter's suggestion, to obtain four tickets for an outing with her and a boyfriend to the Harvard-Yale football game.[11]

Nicholson's initial book for his Boston publishers was a highly entertaining spoof, *The Siege of the Seven Suitors*, which Greenslet had discussed with Nicholson in Indianapolis as early as March 1910 and for which Nicholson signed a publisher's contract soon thereafter (June 23, 1910) in Boston. This agreement provided for the author to receive 15 percent of the retail price (which turned out to be $1.30) for the first twenty-five thousand copies sold, and 20 percent on all sales over twenty-five thousand. Unlike all of his subsequent contracts with Houghton Mifflin, there was no mention of dramatic or motion picture rights, which Nicholson later learned to retain for himself or, if the publishers were involved in soliciting a motion picture commitment, to divide these additional proceeds equally.[12]

It is not clear, apart from dissatisfaction over recent sales and perhaps the slightly higher retail prices Bobbs-Merrill charged ($1.50 for all the early novels), just why Nicholson changed publishers, but he was pleased to establish himself among eastern publishers. In turn, Houghton Mifflin was satisfied with the success of its first Nicholson book, which was also released in England in 1910 and in a Grossett and Dunlap reprint edition in 1912. Uniquely, too, for a Nicholson novel, the American Press Association paid $250 for "exclusive serial rights" for this story, giving the association the right to "publish the said story in serial form to any newspaper or periodical published in the United States and Canada" at any time after June 1, 1911.[13]

Although some reviewers considered the *Siege* narrative a "comedy" that did not reach the quality expected "from so clever a writer handling good material," others were pleased with the "absurdly delightful" tale that involved a wealthy spinster's decision to "marry off" her niece (and heir) and the efforts of would-be suitors to meet the tests placed before them. *The Bookman*'s reviewer called the book "a piece of extreme cleverness . . . well calculated to satisfy the readers of Mr. Nicholson's other volumes [that] contains here and there, in a few of his characters, something a little finer, more unique and altogether better than anything he has previously done."[14]

Interestingly, although in this book, unlike in at least two others (*The Little Brown Jug*, *A Hoosier Chronicle*), Thomas R. Marshall's actions are in no way connected with the story, the work is dedicated to the Indiana governor, a man Nicholson greatly admired and befriended long before he became the state's chief executive. Marshall, known as a wonderful raconteur, had this quality emphasized in Nicholson's "open letter" to him at the head of the book. Nicholson said that in Indiana, "the telling of

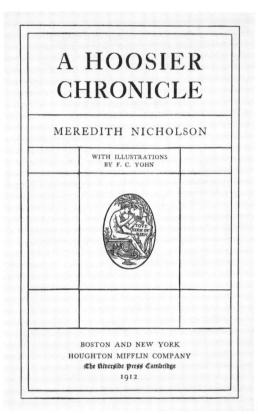

IHS

Cover to Nicholson's A Hoosier Chronicle.

tales [had] brightened the hunter's camp-fire and cheered the lonely pioneer's cabin before our people learned the uses of ink," and that it was of "supreme fitness" to have Marshall as governor because "you are yourself the best of story-tellers." In closing his "unsanctioned writ from that

A SUDDEN FIERCE ANGER BURNED IN HER HEART

IHS

An illustration from A Hoosier Chronicle.

high court of letters in which I am the least valiant among the bailiffs," Nicholson made public his affection for the little man from Columbia City, an attorney whose surprise entrance into the gubernatorial race in 1908 ended in victory. Marshall had defeated the popular James E. Watson, then a member of the U.S. House of Representatives and a future nearly three-term U.S. senator.[15]

In 1913 Nicholson completed, after an extended period of labor, his most significant, and probably his best, novel, *The Hoosier Chronicle*. True to his revised purpose in novel writing, this book was a more serious work, one that looked at life in central Indiana just after the turn of the century and found much to praise as well as much to censure. Nicholson was especially critical of "sharp" business practices and of machine-controlled politics.

The author set the book in his two favorite Indiana cities, Crawfordsville, his birthplace, and Indianapolis, his home base after 1872. As well, this novel's main characters were based more fully upon people he had known in Indianapolis than were any characters in other novels. The model for the book's most intriguing personality, Aunt Sally Owens, the headstrong and outspoken reformer who called not only for women's rights but for many other planks in the "Progressive" platform, was based primarily upon his mother's friend and neighbor, a Mrs. Pattison, and also upon his maternal grandmother, an open-minded, hard-working woman also profiled in *Old Familiar Faces*. Another character, the Reverend John Ware, was clearly a Nicholson tribute to his favorite childhood minister, the Reverend Myron Reed, an advocate and practitioner of muscular Christianity and a thoroughgoing reformer who also read and frequently quoted

Ralph Waldo Emerson, Henry David Thoreau, and Walt Whitman in his sermons.

The story, a factually based analysis of politics and the role of bosses within the legislative process, is told from the viewpoint of Sylvia Garrison, a young woman from Crawfordsville whose grandfather, with whom she lived, was a professor at Madison (Wabash) College. Her mysterious background and connections to two of the most powerful political figures in the state (and to Aunt Sally) after her arrival in the state capital provide the readers with an inside look at Indiana politics during the first decades of the automobile age. Moreover, a key dramatic element involving the selection of a senator (this was still done by the state legislature or, when one party controlled it, by the caucus of that party) to fill a vacancy was based upon events at the onset of Governor Thomas R. Marshall's administration (1909–13).

This was the surprise "nomination" and subsequent election of Benjamin F. Shively by a secret Democratic caucus that required twenty ballots to reach a decision. Shively was one of eight candidates for the position, but the two favorites (John E. Lamb of Terre Haute, Nicholson's choice, and John W. Kern of Indianapolis) cancelled each other out, and the lesser-known Shively was selected. Thomas Taggart, recognized as the boss of Indiana Democrats, was also one of the candidates, but he withdrew early in the race.[16]

After a wedding in the penultimate chapter between Sylvia and her young suitor that represented a union between rival political camps, the novel ended with an unusual "postscript by the chronicler," but Nicholson invited those who would resent such an intrusion to leave and "slam the door." He then tied up otherwise outstanding issues, as he (the novelist) and his neighbor, Mrs. Sally Owen, attended a senate committee hearing on child labor that included testimony from a woman, the daughter of "Boss" Morton Bassett. En route home around the Monument on the Circle, "whose candelabra flooded the plaza with light," they narrowly avoided being run down by a "honking juggernaut," Nicholson's unflattering term for the automobile, and then continued their stroll as Mrs. Owen reflected upon the changes within the area during her lifetime. She liked the newspaper column, "Hoosier Folks at Home," that "gives you a kind of motion-picture show of cloverfields, and children singing in the country schools, and rural free delivery wagons throwing off magazines and newspapers, and the interurban cars cutting slices out of the lonesomeness of the country folks." Owen expressed amazement at how times had changed, adding that it was "all pretty comfortable and cheerful and busy in Indiana, with lots of old-fashioned human kindness flowing round; and it's getting better all the time. And I guess it's always got to be that way, out here in God's country."[17] So much for Nicholson's conversion to realism—he couldn't resist another happy ending.

Allegra Stewart, in her study of the life and the novels of Nicholson, aptly remarked that the book was a mix of "romance and realism," and concluded that overall it "vividly conveyed . . . a record of a decade of real life in Indianapolis." Maxwell Perkins, the legendary editor at Scribner's, wrote in 1920 that Nicholson's "convention chapter" was "by far the best thing of that nature that I ever read anywhere," and confessed to being "ashamed" that he had never read the story before Nicholson became one of Scribner's authors.[18]

The book, despite its length and departure from "standard" Nicholson novels, received good reviews and was extremely popular. In addition to *The House of a Thousand Candles* and its immediate successor, *The Port of Missing Men*, only *A Hoosier Chronicle* appears among the nation's best sellers, according to figures compiled on an annual basis. Nicholson, too, always considered this his best novel, saying, "There is more of the Indiana I have known in that story than in anything else I have written."[19]

As suggested by the main drama analyzed in *Chronicle*, however, Nicholson was becoming more and more deeply involved in and with Indiana politics, and his fame as a writer and speaker continued to grow. He admitted to a "slight involvement" in the Democratic fight over selecting a senator in 1909, but "his man" [Lamb] did not prevail. Nevertheless, his friendship with Marshall, the newly elected governor, continued. Nicholson helped to arrange

*Thomas R. Marshall, who served two terms as vice president
under Woodrow Wilson.*

IHS, BASS PHOTO COMPANY COLLECTION, P130

the gala held immediately following Marshall's inauguration on January 5, 1909; he was with the governor when
the Indiana marker at Antietam was dedicated in 1910 and
again during the formal launching of a drive for a "Greater
Culver" at the Culver Military Academy; and he was also
at Marshall's side when the offer to be Wilson's running
mate in 1912 came.[20] Nicholson also, as he inimitably
stated, "offered myself to be shot at" in the Democratic
primary in 1912, and "was licked by the Taggart crowd, but
we who hope for the elimination of Taggart from Democratic management in this state had the satisfaction of seeing him smoked out in the open convention." This was, he
explained, "the whole aim of Marshall's plan, to make it
impossible for the Republicans in the fall campaign to say
if the Democrats won, Taggart would go to the senate."
Nicholson added that when Lamb, who "used to be in the
Taggart crowd but is now a bitter enemy, stood up before
that big crowd [at the convention] and defied them, I was
reminded of the good old times when Wendell Phillips
didn't consider that he had made a good speech unless he
had been hissed."[21]

Earlier, probably because of his friendship with
James Whitcomb Riley, Nicholson attended the May
1907 Decoration Day reception for President Theodore
Roosevelt at the Indianapolis home of Vice President
Charles W. Fairbanks. The president was in Indianapolis
to speak at the unveiling of the monument to a comrade-

IHS, CHARLES BRETZMAN COLLECTION, P338

Luncheon group with President Theodore Roosevelt
at the home of Vice President Charles Fairbanks.
Nicholson is standing fifth from the left.

in-arms, General Henry W. Lawton, killed in the Philippines during the American occupation following the Spanish-American War. The luncheon, attended by some forty prominent people of the city and state, has passed into political lore because of the perceived, but perhaps unintentional, wide distance between the adjacent chairs of the president and vice president. Some believed this symbolized the political differences of the two men. The often-published photograph of the large bipartisan group there, assembled on the lawn outside of the Fairbanks mansion, reveals the tall, handsome Nicholson standing behind Riley, who was seated on the front row along with Fairbanks, Roosevelt, Governor J. Frank Hanly, and Senator Albert J. Beveridge. Taggart, then the chairman of the National Democratic Committee, was standing behind the president.[22]

Nicholson was becoming a celebrity in his own right, and a number of prestigious honors came his way. In 1908 he was elected to membership in the exclusive American Academy and Institute of Arts and Letters, a group to which Riley had also recently been named and whose members included Mark Twain and William Dean Howells. Robert Underwood Johnson, a longtime friend and fellow poet from Indiana who edited the *Century Magazine*, was Nicholson's chief sponsor for this honor.[23] Nicholson also was called upon in 1911 to introduce Alfred Tennyson Dickens, the son of Charles Dickens, at the closing session of the annual meeting of Indiana State Teachers Association in Tomlinson Hall, after which he took the English visitor to see Riley.[24]

At about this time, too, Nicholson sat for his portrait (for the second time) by Wayman Adams. The still-young artist, a prize student of William Forsyth, one of the major figures in the Hoosier Group of artists and a faculty member at the John Herron School of Art, soon became one of Indiana's most eminent portrait artists. Nicholson was particularly pleased with his second Adams painting and its depiction of him as looking "well fed."[25]

Nicholson had already been recognized by Wabash College and Butler University for his historical book, *The Hoosiers*, with honorary master's degrees in 1901 and 1902, respectively, and Wabash added an honorary doctor of literature degree in 1907. Nicholson also made a second trip to Europe, sailing to England in 1912, this time with Dr. Carleton B. McCulloch, one of his closest long-term friends who was not also a writer. A third companion on this trip was Oscar P. "Pop" Welborn. The men visited London and Oxford and then enjoyed brief sojourns in France, including visits to Paris and Versailles, Germany, and Italy.[26]

McCulloch, the son of the well-known Social Gospel minister Oscar O. McCulloch, who had come to Indianapolis in 1877, became a medical doctor and was the personal physician of both Riley and Nicholson. Their trip seemed to solidify a close relationship between author and doctor, and their correspondence during periods of their physical separation is a veritable treasure trove of information about themselves and their beloved homeland. Moreover, in the 1920s McCulloch was twice the Democratic candidate for governor. In the second campaign in 1924, he was joined by Nicholson who ran for a seat in the Indiana Senate.

Nicholson was also offered the chance, by President Woodrow Wilson, to become the American minister to Portugal in June 1913. An appointment of some kind for Nicholson had long been anticipated by others, he suggested, more than by himself. When the offer became official, the *Indianapolis Star* proudly announced it on the front page of its June 19, 1913, issue. The story, "Nicholson Named United States Envoy to Lisbon," was accompanied by three large photographs, one of the dark-haired, bow-tied author, and another of Eugenie Nicholson and all three of the children. The third picture, on an inside page, was a large view of the house at 1500 North Delaware Street, "one of the most attractive in Indianapolis."[27]

Because of Nicholson's occasional jibes at the Democratic Party machine, this proposed appointment was not universally popular, particularly with Joseph M. Bell, the Democratic nominee for mayor of Indianapolis; Harry Warrum, another Indianapolis leader; and other "Taggart Democrats" who wanted only "loyal" Democrats to be so recognized. Even Claude G. Bowers, later Nicholson's close friend and fellow diplomat in the 1930s, was annoyed at Wilson's choice, made without consultation with the Democratic senators (Bowers was the administrative assistant to one, Senator Kern). Bowers also resented Nicholson's independence in disagreeing, openly and pointedly, with Secretary of State William Jennings Bryan on policy issues, and Bowers, admittedly writing during a time of emotional distress, called Nicholson a "cheap snob," much less deserving of preferment than others.[28]

When pressed for an immediate response to the news of his appointment, which had come in by telegraphic dispatch, Nicholson first expressed surprise. "I can hardly believe it," he said, "I never asked for the place, and things don't generally come to a person unless he asks for them." He then laughingly deflected his questioner's desire for an answer, saying "I can not tell yet," because he wanted to consult with his wife first. She was then en route with the children to Mackinac Island, so an immediate response would be impossible, but he insisted that he had "always been a good Democrat." Then, "changing the subject suddenly," he continued, "People around seemed to be sure that I was going to get that appointment—more sure than I was. During the last few days three persons have come to me wanting to lease our house." He also hinted at the possibility of declining the appointment. In addition to being a "good Democrat," Nicholson added that "I have always been a pretty good Hoosier, and I am not so anxious to go to Portugal as some persons may think." "I am sure that I will enjoy it there," he added diplomatically, "although I have not traveled in the country [and] we have the children to consider." Concerned about their education abroad, he suggested that it could be handled "all right. If they go to the continent, we will make linguists of them."[29]

Nothing further regarding the Portugal appointment appeared in the *Star* until five days later when the headlines told virtually the whole story: "Nicholson Will Not Accept the Post of United States Minister" and "[Nicholson] Gives Domestic Reasons Why He Would Stay Here." Louis Ludlow, the *Star*'s perceptive Washington bureau reporter who later became an Indiana congressman, took pains in his report to emphasize that President Wilson's decision to withdraw Nicholson's name was at Nicholson's own "insistent request," and that "the President has not been influenced to take this step by any criticism of the appointment." And Taggart, who "showed up unexpectedly in Washington this evening" for an unscheduled dinner meeting with Indiana's congressional delegation, declined to comment on Nicholson's decision.[30]

The *Indianapolis News*, an evening paper, carried Nicholson's statement in full regarding his actions that day:

I should like my friends in Indiana to know that I have not been indifferent to the great honor which the President paid me in offering me this position. It is true, as has been said, that I was not an applicant for any position within the gift of the President. I was away from home when the local agitation began over rumors from Washington that I might be appointed to some position, and was a good deal amused to find that some of my fellow-Democrats were displeased at the thought of my recognition. This is the first word I have said on this subject in any way, and I take pleasure in assuring my critics that I have always been a consistent Democrat and a believer in Democratic doctrines. I voted for Mr. Bryan in 1908. I am a forward looking Democrat and believe that Woodrow Wilson represents the highest ideals and best aims of the American people.

I do not feel that Portugal is just now as interesting as America. And I am not anxious to miss the strife and struggle attendant upon the making of Indianapolis into an ideally well governed city. No one can understand how attached I am to Indianapolis, or how high I hope to see her stand among American cities. But my feeling that Lisbon is not a wholly desirable place for my children in their formative years is the chief factor in determining my decision.[31]

In 1913, too, Nicholson served on the grand jury for the U.S. District Court for the District of Indiana, and his fellow jurors chose him as their foreman. No details concerning this service or the "true bills" returned have been discovered, but it demonstrates again his active citizenship and interest in the welfare of his state. So too did concern for Riley, whose health was declining, take a bit of Nicholson's time. Nearly every letter received or sent to friends acquainted with him made mention of the great poet, who had suffered a stroke in 1910 but whose quick recovery while in Florida cheered them all. Still, Nicholson wondered about who put the "rye in Riley" during that time, and he otherwise occupied himself by writing a book about "the poet that everyone loved" as a tribute to his revered friend. Initially titled and contracted for as "The House of Dreams," Nicholson later accepted the publisher's suggestion to change it to simply "The Poet."

The preparation of this book was done in secrecy, both in order to surprise Riley on the occasion of his birthday in 1914 and to prevent a rival publisher (Nicholson worried specifically about Bobbs-Merrill) from anticipating his work with a hasty one of their own. But Nicholson agreed with his Boston editors to try to get Riley's cooperation—by way of a photograph depicting him and Nicholson—in publicizing the book as soon as it appeared. To Nicholson's surprise, the usually shy poet consented to having his photograph taken and seemed clearly touched by the honor under way on his behalf. Of course, *The Poet* (1914) was not a biography of Riley, but the man described in it had some of Riley's characteristics, particularly his love of language and of children. "I think there is a good deal of the old boy in that book," Nicholson told his editors shortly after Riley's death.[32]

The post-"Confessions" years also saw Nicholson becoming more famous in his own right, with more and more biographical and "human interest" stories about him appearing in the national press and magazines. He even found it necessary to rent an office "hideaway" downtown where he could do his work—read and write, and, as he said, sometimes just think—in relative privacy. His office on the fifteenth floor of the Merchants National Bank building, at sixteen floors then the city's tallest building,

Nicholson poses with Hoosier poet Riley.

was very sparsely furnished, with no books save a Bible, an anthology, and dictionaries in three languages. His name did not appear on the door or any place else in the building, and a Boston reporter, trying to meet Nicholson for an interview in 1908, called him "the hardest man to find in all of Indianapolis." At this time, too, Nicholson shared a secretary with Booth Tarkington, who typed the handwritten drafts of their work. Sometimes, Nicholson punched out his own letters on a typewriter, but most often his letters were handwritten in his neat and flowing (except when he was very tired) script. One of his correspondents, Robert Cortes Holliday, however, called Nicholson the "worst typist" in the country.[33] Furthermore, in his book about a visit to his home state and to the city he called Tarkingtonapolis, Holliday confirmed Nicholson's reputation as being hard to find. Once located, Nicholson proved to be most convivial and was especially eager, too, to have his visitor meet the "good gray poet," Riley, whom Nicholson always referred to as "the doctor." Holliday described "Nick" as a "tall, strapping gentleman" who had a definite "Indiana look." Such an attribute was hard to define, for "it looks like an idea. George Ade . . . has it. It is all about the streets of Indianapolis [and] the Indiana State Fair." In describing Nicholson further, Holliday said his manners were "decidedly peaceful, and his movements leisurely. A contemplative person. . . . His judgments appeared to be advanced with an openness to correction. The spectacle of the world appeared to afford him a continuous fund of quiet amusement." Overall, Holliday found him to be "a remarkably friendly sort of cove, with apparently, refreshingly little to do."[34]

Other Nicholson correspondence went to established scholars, particularly at Harvard and Yale; to various literary people, particularly poets; and to ordinary "folks" who wrote him. He answered almost all of his mail and was quite obliging in signing books for his fans and in answering questions about the writing craft. He did not, however, reply to the uninformed person who had addressed an inquiry to Madame Nicholson! Club activities also accounted for a large amount of his correspondence, as he organized programs for the Contemporary Club or arranged for special guests at the University Club, another one of his homes away from home. In late December 1910, when the prestigious American Historical Association held its annual convention in Indianapolis, Nicholson, as president of the University Club, corresponded with Professor Max Farrand, the distinguished Yale scholar and foremost authority on the Constitutional Convention in Philadelphia in 1787, the records of which he compiled and published in a definitive four-volume set. Nicholson arranged for Farrand, an officer of the association, and other "wise men of the East" to dine at the University Club during the convention. Nicholson also mentioned to Farrand that one of his former colleagues, the prolific and versatile scholar William G. Sumner, had "stayed with us" a few years ago.[35]

Nicholson also played a leading role in the observation, by Indiana officials and citizens, of the state's centennial in

1916. In addition to updating his book, *The Hoosiers*, for which he wrote a new concluding chapter in 1915, he took the helm in planning a "Return to Indiana Day," an attempt to have famous former Hoosiers come back to their home state—and many did. This was also a feather in the cap of Governor Samuel M. Ralston, with whom Nicholson worked closely over the months. Additionally, when called upon to speak at various times, Nicholson presented his ideas on a favorite theme, *Style and the Man* (1911).[36] During the war years, of course, he developed new, more timely material for talks on the current crisis, and he frequently contributed patriotic pieces to the local press.

These years were also marked by sadness. In July 1915, after a long illness while residing with her son and his family, Emily Meredith Nicholson, the author's mother, died at the age of seventy-three. The front-page notice of her death described her as "a woman of unusual intellectual ability and literary judgment. She was deeply interested in public affairs and was a reader of newspapers as well as books." Her only son discovered, upon going through her papers, that his mother had collected and stored every scrap of his writings. This, he said, touched him deeply, and he went on to say, in a sentiment similar to Abraham Lincoln's praise for his mother, that "a good deal of what I know I learned from her."[37]

Almost exactly a year later, Riley, Nicholson's mentor and perhaps his closest friend, also died. The previous fall, on October 7, 1915, Nicholson had organized a huge sixty-sixth birthday celebration for Riley that turned out to be his last. Scores of people either showed up in person or sent written tributes to the great poet, whose memory is now perpetuated through the Riley Hospital for Children, one of the nation's most outstanding such facilities. Nicholson was one of the charter members of the Riley Memorial Association, which promoted the hospital's creation. Yet, as Nicholson told a Boston friend, "I miss Riley and shall always miss him," and he often commented that the "town doesn't seem the same without him."[38]

The onset of World War I in 1914 also led to enormous and enormously significant labors by Nicholson and his family. They were actively involved in the war relief and civilian defense programs, and Nicholson, as one of the leaders of the drive for preparedness, made frequent addresses and wrote articles on behalf of the Allies. The family had a hand in organizing the "Lawton Guards," a paramilitary organization in which Nicholson's youngest child, Lionel ("Tookie"), served as the recruiting officer. Nicholson wrote to a friend, evidently with pride, that "Tookie" had beaten up a young boy of German ancestry whose derogatory comments about the United States had infuriated the young Nicholson.[39]

The elder Nicholsons did their "war work" in different ways. Meredith later quipped that "he killed the Kaiser daily with his typewriter," as his countless addresses and articles all supported the war and probably contributed to the anti-German feelings that peaked during this time. Such attitudes led to the renaming of Das Deutsche Haus as the Athenaeum and stopped the publication of German-language newspapers in the city and the teaching of the language in the local schools. Some commonly used items also received new names, as "sauerkraut," for example, became "liberty cabbage."[40]

Eugenie Nicholson was particularly active in her role as a Red Cross volunteer, traveling to Chicago upon occasions, and she worked, as did her sister-in-law, Margaret Nicholson Noble, on various other relief causes. Locally the citizens of Marion County donated as much as $500,000 to the Red Cross, and they also oversubscribed all the Liberty Loans. The drive for the fourth Liberty Loan in October 1918, with Marion County's quota set at $23.4 million, yielded well over $24 million.

In April 1917, upon the eve of the United States' entry into the war, Nicholson addressed a "monster" rally on Monument Circle, at which he presented a series of resolutions that he had drawn up calling for American entry into the war. These were adopted, sent to Washington, and, to Nicholson's surprise and delight, incorporated with almost no change into President Wilson's momentous address to Congress asking for a declaration of war.[41] When Nicholson wrote to a confidant in Boston about the rally, "a regular whopper," he said that he had read his resolutions

IHS, BASS PHOTO COMPANY COLLECTION, P130

Nicholson prepares to address a group of Indiana soldiers who had just returned from World War I at the Severin Hotel in Indianapolis. Nicholson (on the right) is one of two men in civilian clothing standing in front of the stage at the far end of the room.

"in a voice that all the Middle West must have heard." He added the shocking detail that, when he "stood up before the four thousand to read," he was armed with a pistol—"a 32 carelessly lying in my right hand coat pocket"—and that he did not "feel dressed without my gun these days—so many hyphenates aruound [*sic*] you never can tell when you'll have to pop one," and he later cried out in a letter, "On to Berlin! Germany must be utterly destroyed."[42] Obviously he had come to believe his own propaganda, and he supported the war effort with more than words. Using his euphemism of "needing shoes for his children" when he was low in funds, he told editor Scaife in early

November 1917 that "I am in some need of shoes. The Americans took a hundred dollars from me yesterday—the hat is passed here every hour."[43]

Throughout these events, Nicholson somehow maintained his usual writing, issuing, after the appearance of *The Lords of High Decision* (1912), a second book (of essays) that year, and one book each year for the rest of the decade, except for 1915 and 1917, when again there were two. The book of essays, *The Provincial American*, was a collection of previously published articles, and the novels included this author's favorite one, *Otherwise Phyllis* (1913), set in Crawfordsville; *The Poet* (1914), published in concert with Riley's sixty-fifth birthday; *The Proof of the Pudding* (1916); *The Madness of May* (1917); and *A Reversible Santa Claus* (1917). The last three books all stemmed from magazine serials that Nicholson placed in *Redbook* and *Collier's* and were basically light romances, even fantasies. His next book, however, was his most serious and significant piece of work since *A Hoosier Chronicle*. It too was a series of articles, not a novel, and was an in-depth look at mid-America, its attitudes, and its values. Worked out in detail with editor Maxwell Perkins and to be called, at the editor's suggestion, *The Valley of Democracy*, this assignment required Nicholson to travel and investigate life in the broad "valley" between Ohio and Nebraska, with a special look at its main city, Chicago, the subject of one of the six articles or chapters. Perceptive and informative, powerful and direct, and told from the perspective of one who had intimate knowledge and feeling for the region, *Valley of Democracy* ranks with *The Hoosiers* as a valuable book. It also contains much of Nicholson's philosophy of life, his belief in democracy, democratic values, and the goodness and good-naturedness of the "folks" who populated the "valley of democracy."

Happily, too, the book was well received, and Nicholson felt his time and effort in producing the articles, first published in *Scribner's Magazine* between January and June 1918, and then released as a single volume in September, were well spent. The good reception given the book was not universal. In particular, Randolph Bourne, who reviewed the book for *Dial Magazine*, also did a fuller essay on the Middle West and its portrayers, including, most prominently, Nicholson. His complaint regarding Nicholson was his myopia regarding the people there. Nicholson, he charged, had "but one class . . . in mind—his own, the prosperous people of the towns." He was dismissive of the farmers and overlooked completely the workers in the mills and mines.[44] Another light-hearted Nicholson novel, *Lady Larkspur*, appeared in 1919, thus ending a decade of remarkable productivity, of gains and losses.[45] He was ready for more activity, productivity, and joie de vivre in the 1920s.

8

The Madness of May

*"'The Madness of May.' That's one of the drollest books ever written.
A story like that is a boon to mankind; it kept me chuckling
all night. . . . Along about this season it's in the blood of healthy
human beings to pine for clean air and the open road.
It's the wanderlust that's in all of us, old and young alike."*[1]
MEREDITH NICHOLSON, 1917

ALTHOUGH MEREDITH NICHOLSON'S BOOK OF THIS NAME,
The Madness of May (a story about a book—a fairy tale—
of the same name), was written and published as a series
of articles in 1916 and as a book in 1917, it serves here as
a description of Nicholson's hectic but still happy and productive life in the 1920s.

Overall, for Nicholson, the 1920s involved significant transitions—the marriage of his three children, in
1920, 1925, and 1929; the move from the place on North
Delaware Street, still known as the House of a Thousand
Candles, into an apartment, temporarily, and then to
Golden Hill; and finally the move (in 1930) to an elegant
home on North Meridian Street, next door to Kin Hubbard, whose untimely passing soon afterwards deprived
Nicholson of another close friend and fellow author.[2]
In addition, the decade marked Nicholson's first serious
run for public office (the state senate) as an outspoken

opponent—and hence an unsuccessful candidate—of the Ku Klux Klan in 1924. The Klan was then at the height of its power and influence in the state, and Nicholson's courageous criticism of its excesses, joined in by his friend and physician, Carleton B. McCulloch, the Democratic candidate for governor, earned him more notoriety around the nation.[3]

Moreover, as the 1920s wore on, Nicholson remained deeply involved in politics, particularly at the local level as a critic of the Klan-influenced city administration headed by Mayor John Duvall. When Duvall and most members of the city council were forced to resign, Nicholson was appointed (not elected) to fill out an unexpired term on the council. "Hell's bells," he complained to David L. Chambers, "I'm in public office!" Yet Nicholson felt obligated, in view of his criticism of others, to accept the appointment and do his best.[4]

This new commitment carried a heavy price—its considerable demands denied Nicholson the time and the solitude he needed in order to write. Of course, many other factors were involved too, but after the 1920s Nicholson never again published an imaginative book or story. At first, however, his writings continued, and his work moved into the realm of social problems, especially the alarming increase in divorce. Nicholson was also concerned about the lowered tone of life among the younger generation, and he once considered doing a book on the "The Ris-

In advising young writers, Nicholson urged them to
"stay in your own home town."

ing Tide of Vulgarity in America." Throughout the 1920s
Nicholson produced five novels, two books of essays, one
collection of short stories, and a play, thus maintaining his
normal rate of doing just under one book a year. He also

produced a large amount of miscellaneous writings—book introductions, published speeches, and even a brief campaign biography of former Indiana governor Samuel R. Ralston, whose presidential campaign in 1928 was also brief.

Many of Nicholson's writings during this time first appeared in magazines, for which he received large checks, and later came out in book form, and some of his social commentaries attracted considerable comment in letters to the editor (and to the author). While the reactions to his writings in the 1920s were less public than in the decade before, they were nonetheless substantial, and it took considerable time for the author to answer them.

Regretfully, the reception given to Nicholson's "problem" novels was unenthusiastic both in terms of sales and critical comment. Reviewers still praised the writer's lucid, graceful style and his ingenious, if improbable, plotting, but his attempts at realism too often gave way in the end to implausible outcomes. His first book of this decade, *Black Sheep! Black Sheep!* (1920), had his protagonist, unassertive and very proper socially, undertake a house-hunting errand to Maine for his sister and, in the process, shoot and possibly kill an intruder. His flight as a fugitive brought him into contact with "The Professor," a well-read and well-spoken criminal and bootlegger. Their escapades and chance meetings with acquaintances all across the eastern half of the United States and the fugitive's eventual return to the good

graces and embraces of his true love provide an enticing, if
fanciful, look at the underworld as seen by Nicholson. But
he admitted to knowing nothing about criminals and said
he probably couldn't write about them if he did. Still, the
New York Times called the book "breathlessly contrived
and as diverting to follow as a crooked street in a mediaeval
town, along which anything might happen."[5]

Nicholson followed this book with *The Man in the
Street* (1921), a collection of essays on politics, society,
and letters, including his thoughtful and most complete
essay on the life and work of James Whitcomb Riley. This
article, like most of the others, had first appeared in the
Atlantic Monthly and had been rewritten five or six times
until Nicholson was at last satisfied with it. He remained
pleased with this view of Riley ever after, and he often said
that the essay gave "a very fair idea of the poet" he knew
intimately for many years.[6]

Another timely essay here, written just after the disappointing 1916 election, was his piece on the "Second Rate
Man in Politics," lamenting the dearth of viable candidates
in both parties "fit" for public office and the "geographical
limitations" in effect that had excluded candidates from
New England, the South, and as yet the trans-Mississippi
West. He also decried the prevalence of "second-rate"
men in all levels of government. "Politics," he charged,
unlike business, "puts a premium upon inferiority," particularly in municipal government, where, since "first rate

men are not 'available' for the office, they naturally fall
to the inferior, the incompetent, or the corrupt." Nicholson concluded with a call for "first-rate men to undertake
offices of responsibility and power."[7]

There were ten essays in *The Man in the Street*, includ-
ing Nicholson's demand that eastern urbanites "Let Main
Street Alone"; his provocative piece, "How, Then, Should
Smith Vote?"; and another one of his many pleas for high
standards in grammar, "The Poor Old English Language."
The *New York Times* reviewer praised the author's belief
in folks, for he is one of the "folksiest of them all," and he
"prods them to meet their responsibilities in a democracy."
Other reviewers, more openly critical than before, speared
Nicholson's pretensions and deplored his ethnocentrism,
and one uncharitably concluded that, although Nicholson
"always says some perfectly agreeable and true things," he
"always stops short of saying anything important." Another
wondered why these pieces had been "culled" from the
magazines at all.[8]

As if mindful of these criticisms, Nicholson's next
book, *Best Laid Schemes* (1922), was his only collection
of short stories, a genre he professed to know little about,
but the stories gathered here are varied, interesting, fast-
paced, and engrossing. Although one character, Webster
G. Burgess of the White River National Bank, is in three
of the stories, each is complete in itself. Reviewers rated
the volume as "consistently entertaining," affording a fine

way "to while away an idle hour or two."[9] The six tales
in the collection are "The Susiness of Susan"; "The Girl
with the Red Feather"; "The Campbells Are Coming";
"Arabella's House Party"; "The Third Man"; and "Wrong
Number." Nicholson selected "The Third Man" for inclusion in *My Story That I Liked Best*, compiled and edited
by Ray Long, the longtime editor of *Cosmopolitan*. It was
something of a mystery story that turned on the distinctive doodles of one of the men attending a meeting, which
matched those found on a scrap of paper at the scene of a
crime. The meeting, of course, was a trap, with every place
at the table having a tablet and pencil provided, and the
supposedly innocent doodles of one of the attendees did
indeed serve to identify the perpetrator.[10]

Nicholson's return to a problem novel, *Broken Barriers* (also 1922), continued to displease his critics. In a
story set again in Indianapolis, the heroine is one of the
"new women" of the 1920s who tries to make her way as
a sales clerk after being forced to leave the state university for financial reasons. Her attraction to an unhappily
married man could not be fulfilled, despite the "broken
barriers" of many social conventions, until after the fortuitous accidental death of the man's older wife. "None of
these things are impossible, but they are so unusual that
they cannot convince," complained one reviewer. Another
disliked Nicholson's "woeful" mix-up of his materials "in
the realm of pseudo-realism."[11]

"There is nothing of itself important in sex and drunks except what the artist can lend them of human interest and significance," said a third reviewer, concluding that "Mr. Nicholson lends them nothing, not even the covering of a good style." The minority opinion was that, even though Nicholson "may have flinched from the task he set for himself" by providing an improbable happy ending, the book's "vivid portraiture of character" made "much of it a delight," and that, said another, "as in all of his stories, Mr. Nicholson's diction is smooth, his sense of proportion admirable, and his reasoning logical."[12]

Certainly the editor of *Cosmopolitan*, to whom Nicholson originally had submitted his manuscript, was most enthusiastic about it, and he trumpeted the virtues of the eight-part series to the magazine's readers. Asking the questions, "Are American girls different [today] . . . ? If they are, what changed them? And will they be better for the change, or worse?" the editor (Long) then suggested that "Mr. Nicholson has molded this subject into one of the most vital novels we have ever published" and asserted that "We believe you will find here that he has done the most brilliant work of his career." Others have compared Nicholson's *Broken Barriers* favorably with Tarkington's contemporaneous *Alice Adams* (1921), which also dealt with the life of a single working girl in the big city and which won for Tarkington his second Pulitzer Prize, but most recognize that Nicholson tempered his realism, whereas Tarkington's "realism [was] unalloyed by sentimentality."[13]

When Nicholson entered new ground with what he called the "social problem" novel, he admittedly was not a big fan of the genre. Yet he worried about weakening standards of conduct and the lower moral tone that had seemed to occur at the beginning of Prohibition. He decided to try his hand at realistic critiques of contemporary American life, particularly infidelity and divorce, even among the so-called better class of people. *Broken Barriers* was his first such work, which was followed by the *Hope of Happiness* (1922), but his most ambitious novel of this type was his hard-hitting *And They Lived Happily Ever After* (1925).

The genesis of this book was another book of a special kind—the large alimony book maintained in the Marion County Clerk's office. Nicholson had first become aware of books of this type during his service as a jury commissioner, when he had occasion often to visit the clerk's office. He witnessed a steady stream of women, "of all sorts and conditions, who came in and signed this book, received cash or a check and departed." Seeing so many "beneficiaries" and such a large receipt book set Nicholson to "thinking a great deal about the stability of marriage." Then, after considerable investigation, he undertook a second "problems" book. "My purpose in writing *And They Lived Happily Ever After* was to picture a condition that is quite typical with a view to encouraging discussion and perhaps doing a little good," he told an *Indianapolis Star* reporter. "Everywhere the increase of divorce is appalling . . . [But], as Mark Twain said about the weather, everybody talks about the divorce evil but nobody does anything." He said he set the scene in Indianapolis because "I know—or think I know—its history, and have studied with attention the interesting social changes that have been perceptible ever since the first automobiles ran over our streets."[14]

Nicholson's study here of the properly and improperly entwined lives of two couples was intended as a "composite of a hundred instances of unhappy marriages" and his solution—eventual remarriage of the central figures, the Conners, after a brief, unsatisfying taste of "freedom"— did not please all his critics, but the novel enjoyed modest success and perhaps stimulated some discussion of the problem. Indeed, Nicholson said that he wanted the book to be an "irritant" to the complacent, and he hoped the "pulpits and social agencies around the country would address the issues, too."

Ironically, there is now some evidence to suggest that Nicholson came to know personally, better than he wanted to admit, a great deal about secret love affairs and infidelity. Many believe, as two cryptic letters years later perhaps confirm, that Nicholson had an adulterous relationship with Ruth Watson, one of his secretaries, during the 1920s, when Eugenie Nicholson was ill for extended periods and during which time Nicholson continued to work at his unmarked downtown office. It is known that Watson assisted Nicholson in his later works, "helping" him dress his female characters appropriately for the times. Moreover, biographer Allegra Stewart, who was also a friend of the Nicholson family, flatly asserts that Ruth Watson was his mistress; another friend once quipped that Nicholson lived his life backwards, sowing his wild oats late in life; and a son came to believe that his father had been unfaithful.[15]

Perhaps Nicholson's relationship with another secretary, his last one before starting his diplomatic service, also involved more than met the eye, because just before he left the country for South America, Nicholson abruptly married her, and she was with him during all of his years as a U.S. Minister abroad. Most assuredly, the rest of the Nicholson family did not "approve" of the new Mrs. Nicholson and resented her elevated status as family matriarch. Years later, in a wide-ranging oral history interview, daughter-in-law Roberta West Nicholson, when asked about the new Mrs. Nicholson and where she had come from, expressed considerable animosity toward Dorothy Wolfe Lannon Nicholson and answered the origins question variously, saying either "from under a rock" or "from the woodwork." As well, about all Roberta's son, who was not yet seven years old at the time of his grandfather's second wedding, remembers about his step-grandmother is that she had "big lips and an enormous bosom."[16]

The most direct evidence regarding Watson and her supposed relationship with Nicholson, however, comes from Roberta's recollections. During transcribed interviews in 1983, she said that Watson, in about 1927 or 1928, decided to take her employer to court. She claimed that she had "written his books" and was his long-time "lover," and she wanted additional compensation. The family, obviously distressed, discussed the situation, and Eugenie asked her daughter-in-law, Roberta, to call upon Watson and "talk some sense into her." During her visit in Watson's apartment, Roberta noticed some men's clothing, not Nicholson's, in the closet, so she added the threat of exposing her promiscuity to the basic point that Nicholson had produced his best novels long before she worked for him and that her claims of authorship were unfounded. This visit, she said, "called her bluff" and ended Watson's plans for a lawsuit.[17]

Later, in 1932, Watson tried to reestablish contact with the recently widowed Nicholson, suggesting they meet and bring their "stupid" quarrel to an end, because "we were identified with each other for a great many years," and since "Indianapolis is a small town," it had its "share of small-town curiosity about its citizens." There is no known response to this letter, and a few months later a second letter from a Marie Watson in Chicago, whose relationship to Ruth is not clear, bluntly asked Nicholson for money, "any amount you can spare," sent to General

Cover of Nicholson's The Cavalier of Tennessee.

Delivery, Chicago. But nothing further along these lines developed.[18]

As a survey of his publications indicates, Nicholson's output for the decade of the 1920s was "frontloaded"— only the semibiographical novel about Andrew and Rachel Jackson and the collection of partly biographical (and autobiographical) essays in *Old Familiar Faces*

(1929) appeared after 1925, and these were his last books. The Jackson book, titled *The Cavalier of Tennessee* (1928), was a highly factual but romanticized biographical study of the prepresidential years of Jackson's life, particularly his courtship and marriage, under highly unusual circumstances, to Rachel Donelson Robards. Published on July 4, 1928, the book represented more than three years of intensive research work by Nicholson. Tragically, as many know, Rachel, whose untidy marital status became an issue in the presidential campaign of 1828, died between the time of Jackson's election and his inauguration (a death that Jackson blamed upon his political opponents, taking certain steps in retaliation). But Nicholson's focus was on the early life of the young couple, pioneers in the Tennessee wilderness where Rachel was born and where Jackson (a Carolina native) entered upon his ambitious legal, military, and political career. Surprisingly accurate in its command of the details, the book sold well and became one of Nicholson's all-time favorite works.[19]

It now seems appropriate that Nicholson's last novel dealt with politics, because increasingly through the 1920s his own life was more and more deeply involved in political campaigns, either managing or participating in them, while also writing about politics. Indeed, there were literally dozens of short pieces in the latter 1920s on politics and society that kept Nicholson's name before the public and his coffers supplied.

Examples of other miscellaneous publications in the 1920s are a number of book introductions, including the special one previously mentioned and quoted at length above (in the introduction) for Kin Hubbard's *Book of Indiana* (1929); and biographical sketches of artist Franklin Booth, who had illustrated some of Nicholson's books, and friends Carleton B. McCulloch, Evans Woollen, and William Fortune, the latter upon the occasion of the tenth anniversary celebration of his founding of the Indianapolis chapter of the American Red Cross. There were even contributions to a cookbook ("Wabash Valley Steak") and most surprisingly, perhaps, a sports column in the *Indianapolis News* in March 1929. Sports editor William F. Fox Jr. had to be away for a day, so he asked Nicholson to fill in for him.

It happened to be at the time of the Indiana high school basketball tournament and resulted in a most unusual sports commentary, one that made occasional historical references to the communities the teams represented and offered but little on the games in the Butler Fieldhouse beyond revealing the author's biases. "It tickles me that [Indianapolis] Tech knocked the persimmons today in the scramble with Vincennes," he wrote. "The Tech grounds soaked up a lot of history in old times. It is proper the boys should win victories." Nicholson's report on an earlier contest stated only that "Rushville seems to have won this game, 28–24. But I salute Winamac's first citizen, Lermond Stout," who reminded Nicholson of Olympian athletes. He reserved most of the space in his column for comments on the evening finale between Muncie in Delaware County and Washington in Daviess County, a team with two African American players, which won the game, 31–24: "Even a rube like me knows it was a great game." Finally, the erstwhile sportswriter suggested that "this tremendous interest in basketball is significant of the good cheer and moral health of the Hoosier people. . . . [It's] wholesome to have something to think about besides bandits, bootleggers and political crookedness."[20]

Nicholson also published nine articles in the *American Legion Monthly* between 1926 and 1929 and a host of articles (including serialized versions of four novels) in *Cosmopolitan* (later combined with *Hearst International*) magazine, and a large number of his speeches were carried in full in the local press. Certainly Nicholson's name continued to appear before the American public in this decade, and he was signally honored for his productivity and his citizenship by Indiana University in 1928. "Meredith Nicholson," proclaimed President William Lowe Bryan as he awarded the coveted honorary doctor of laws degree, "You are novelist. You are poet. You are patriot. You are soldier in the trenches fighting to redeem your city and state from shame. These are titles to honor greater than any academic dignity. Go back to your trenches. Perhaps there in the thick of the fight you will find and write your greatest poem."[21]

There was an irony in receiving this recognition at that time. Unknown to all at the time, Nicholson's career as a writer was over. In part, the absence of new novels and other imaginative writings represented a drying up of his creative juices. When Nicholson regretfully declined an invitation to take part in a Christmas symposium, he admitted to self-doubt: "I have lost my knack, if I ever had any, of knocking off a few paragraphs, even on easy subjects. It would take a month to say what I would like to say about Christmas, and it wouldn't be the right stuff."[22]

Another reason for Nicholson's comparative meager output was a growing involvement in politics. Such an interest was not new, stemming, indeed, from his childhood and always somewhat alarming to his literary friends, such as Riley, who feared the political siren would lure Nicholson away from the literary muses. Riley expressed his views inimitably in a rhyme he made for the author's son, Meredith Nicholson Jr., on the occasion of the little boy's birthday:

Though you're <u>little</u>, you must know
How we all want you to grow—
    Not to merely five-foot six,
But, at least to six foot clear,—
That you may pull father-dear
    Out of politics.[23]

Such entreaties failed to work; Nicholson's political activism continued to grow over the years. His career in politics had begun, in one sense, when he "jumped the traces" of the family's Republican traditions in 1884 and actively supported Grover Cleveland in his first successful campaign for the presidency in 1884, a race in which the Cleveland ticket included a Hoosier, Thomas A. Hendricks. Hendricks was the hard-luck loser with Samuel J. Tilden in 1876, despite the Tilden-Hendricks team having won a majority of the popular vote. Hendricks had also been a presidential hopeful in 1880 and 1884 before reluctantly accepting the second spot again in the latter year. There is no known contact between the young Democratic convert and his famous fellow Hoosier, although Nicholson knew the man from afar and wrote of him admiringly in different essays. Perhaps the presence of Hendricks on the national ticket in 1884 helped Nicholson in the battle with his family over his new political stance.[24]

Nicholson never desired a political office for himself, although he did consent a time or two to let his name be put in nomination for local office, knowing all the while that he would not be elected or have to serve. The country was then operating in the "system of 1896," which referred to Republican control of almost all the levers of power in the nation. This domination lasted from the 1890s until 1932, or from William McKinley through Herbert Hoover. The Republican hold on the White House was broken only when a split within the party in 1912 paved the way for Woodrow Wilson's two terms as president.[25]

It was a different story in 1924 when the man who was probably his closest friend following the death of Riley was the Democratic candidate for governor. At McCulloch's request, Nicholson consented to run that year for a seat in the state senate, and the two men frequently campaigned together in what was a particularly bitter and divisive contest. As is well known, the Indiana Ku Klux Klan controlled the local and statewide elections.[26] All anti-Klan candidates went down in defeat that year, but in a surprising after-

IHS. P411

Members of the Godfrey Klan, Number 93, in Hartford City, Indiana, pose in their full regalia.

math, soon the Klan itself was defeated as Klan leader D. C. Stephenson was convicted in 1925 on criminal charges of rape and manslaughter. The Klan declined and temporarily disappeared. Newly elected state leaders from the governor on down were implicated in the scandal, but most escaped severe sanctions. Not so, however, in Indianapolis, where the mayor and most members of the city council were convicted on "corrupt practices" charges.[27]

In a retrospective article about the "queer madness" that gripped the state in the 1920s, Nicholson observed that the Klan's decline had come with "disconcerting abruptness," and he rejoiced that this thing "alien to . . . Indiana" had disappeared and that again "bed clothes were used for legitimate purposes." Nicholson credited a Republican editor of Vincennes, Tom Adams, for first having the courage to speak out and help end "the vulgar Kluxing of Indiana." Under "the dictation of th[at] smooth rogue," Stephenson had taken over "a great political party and ruined it with the insolence of a Nero" and Nicholson gloated over the current fate—imprisonment—of the "old man" who had "declared himself to be the law in Indiana" and who once, "with a pistol strapped to his hip, had paraded the aisles of a republican state convention giving orders that had to be obeyed." At the same time, Nicholson lamented the silence of Hoosier authors—namely George Ade, Booth Tarkington, and Kin Hubbard, Republicans all—regarding the Klan, and he worried that the decline "of Hoosier letters suffered by reason of these [Klan] proceedings" might be permanent. Finally, after a gibe at incumbent U.S. Senator James Watson, who testified that "he had seen nothing and he knew nothing," Nicholson jokingly suggested that Stephenson be called upon to write the platform of the Republican State Committee to announce the party's "base desertion" of Stephenson. But Nicholson believed that there was reason to hope, and that "Indiana is gaining her self respect and is showing signs of a healthy return to reason. The poet, teller of tales, and philosopher who had fled to the peace of the hills are again tottering into the post office with sacks of manuscripts."[28]

In addition to the changes in his writings and his increased political involvement at this time, Nicholson's family life also underwent many alterations in the 1920s. The departure from the homestead of two children (through marriage and college) left the Nicholsons with "too much house." Accordingly, late in 1920, the Delaware Street House of a Thousand Candles was sold, with possession changing hands on January 13, 1921, shortly after the marriage of daughter Elizabeth to Benjamin Claypool. The move also allowed Nicholson to indulge his desire "to live in the country," as he evidently then considered suburban Indianapolis. For the moment, however, as Nicholson told a friend in Boston, "we have become cliff dwellers." The Nicholsons moved into a high-rise apartment on Meridian Street, where they lived until they moved into a lovely smaller home on the north side in Golden Hill, along the old Central Canal and just west of the spot where Riley lay at rest atop the crown of Crown Hill Cemetery. Golden Hill, a relatively new upscale suburb, was the brainchild of industrialist David M. Parry, and the Nicholsons lived there throughout much of the 1920s.[29]

Regrettably, because of the absence of family papers, very little is known about family life within the Nicholson home. Some records generated by the eldest son, "Med" (Meredith Nicholson Jr.), along with invaluable recorded interviews of his wife, Roberta West Nicholson, provide most of what is known about the Nicholsons' home life. The eldest son, Med, was a popular, fun-loving boy, and something of a "Penrod" character whose life did not at all resemble the serious, hard-working life of his father as a boy, but he had his father's charm and was tall, good-looking, and gregarious. And he was not a model citizen; at fourteen he was, like both of his parents, a smoker, a habit his father urged him at least to postpone. As the boy noted in his diary in the fall of 1916, "Father promises me a car next spring if I don't smoke till school is out. I got a week to stop [and] only smoked five today. Won $1.50 shooting craps."[30]

Despite his father's encouragement and his mother's example, Med's academic record was not distinguished, but creditable. After beginning at Shortridge High School, he moved to the Taft School, a preparatory school in Watertown, Connecticut, and then to the Milford School, also in

Connecticut, where he completed his secondary education. There is no record of his parents' reaction to his "election" in 1921 by his classmates as Milford School's "biggest bluffer," or as the winner, not only of the first place but also the second and third place prizes, as the school's "laziest"! It goes without saying, given these distinctions, that he was not on any of the sports teams at Milford, though he was also recognized as the class's "wittiest" and "most original thinker." A repeat winner in those categories in 1922, Nicholson, upon graduation that year, was admitted to Yale University, where he remained for about a year before returning home to enter business and to get married.[31]

Even less is known about Elizabeth, the eldest child, and Charles "Tookie," the youngest, neither of whom attended college. Elizabeth, according to her sister-in-law Roberta's recollections, was known as a "social butterfly," did not read much, and loved to travel. When Tookie was about eight years old, he contracted a severe case of scarlet fever, which turned the Nicholson house into something like a hospital ward, with no visitors allowed, not even the siblings, who either went on a trip to California (Med) or to a summer camp (Elizabeth). Later, in the mid-1920s, Tookie became ill again while in Paris. Elizabeth volunteered to go over to help him, but she developed a "shipboard romance," and after briefly visiting with Tookie, disappeared for a time with her Belgian friend.[32] Both of these children, as noted, married in the 1920s. Elizabeth's marriage to Claypool produced a child, Virginia, before a divorce in December 1927. She remarried in August 1932, during the Democratic National Convention, becoming the wife of Austin H. Brown.[33] Tookie was often ill, but he helped organize the Lawton Guards during World War I. In his adult years, although his health problems continued, he married Edith Watson in 1929, and they had a daughter, Jane, in 1933, while Charles, no longer known as Tookie, worked as an insurance agent with the Massachusetts Mutual Life Insurance Company.[34]

Other information about the elder Nicholsons' home life, apart from the joys and trials of parenthood, is that theirs was comparatively a rather leisurely life, with an array of servants—maids, cooks, gardeners, chauffeurs—at hand, although Eugenie, when well, did some of the housework and enjoyed gardening, too. But she was often ill and bedridden. Her daughter-in-law adored "Mother Nicholson," whom she called "the most wonderful woman I ever knew." Eugenie was highly educated (spoke four languages), witty, cultured, and an enormous help to her husband in his literary efforts. It would be wrong, Roberta insisted, to credit the wife with having written Nicholson's books, as some later suggested, but she provided very important assistance to him in his writing. Roberta remembered seeing Nicholson often having morning coffee with his bedridden wife while they discussed plots and scenes and the upcoming day's work for the writer. In particular, Roberta believed

Eugenie helped her husband with finding the Shakespeare quotations that he used in his books.

Nicholson, for his part, although he said he'd like to live in the country, was strictly "an urban man"—he loved to walk, but only on paved surfaces, not on paths through woods or on sandy beaches. He also wore only tailored suits and preferred having others do menial tasks for him. He didn't drive a car, order his own train tickets, or make his own hotel reservations. Of course he kept busy, but his was a life of the mind and the pen (rarely the typewriter) and conversation. He was cordial, always dignified, and reveled in witty repartee.[35]

In October 1925, while the Nicholsons were living in Golden Hill, their elder son, Meredith Jr., married the beautiful and accomplished Roberta West of Cincinnati. The Wests were a leading family of that meat- producing center, where Robert West Jr., Med's new father-in-law, headed the Cincinnati operations of the Hartford Life Insurance Company. Earlier he had founded, as a subsidiary of the company, the Hartford Live Stock Insurance Company, the first one in the nation, and the family prospered as his idea of insuring livestock in transit to market proved very lucrative. The Wests had homes in Ohio, Kentucky, and Florida. The place in Kentucky was a horse-breeding farm, and in 1928 Robert West, despite his wife's disapproval of racing and its inevitable association with the pari-mutuels, entered a horse, Typhoon, in the Kentucky Derby.[36]

The newlyweds had met in northern Michigan (Northport), where both families often spent their summers. They became friends and then betrothed, but their wedding was delayed while young Nicholson completed his formal education and entered business. The marriage was significant in a number of ways. It brought Roberta not only into the Nicholson family, but also into the Democratic Party, to the displeasure, if not the horror, of the West family. The young woman quickly established herself as a social activist deeply committed to the party and to the values of her distinguished (and highly pleased) father-in-law, who also delighted in his grandchildren, first a girl, Virginia, born to Elizabeth and Benjamin Claypool, and then Meredith III and Eugenie, the children of Roberta and Meredith Nicholson Jr.[37]

The "May Madness" decade ended twice for Nicholson, both times abruptly and tragically. The stock market collapse in October 1929 had a devastating impact upon the Nicholsons, even though they carried through on their move into a new home at 5417 North Meridian Street in 1930, having already committed themselves to the transaction. But their time there was not to last very long, or to survive the second sudden ending of the decade and the author's charmed life up to this time. In late December 1931, following recurrent illnesses and long periods of confinement, Eugenie suddenly became seriously ill and died on December 21.[38] Nicholson's life changed, and he faced an uncertain future—no affordable home, no job, and no ability to write.

9

The Land of the Tall Poinsettia

"I admit at once the incompetence of the title as a description of Paraguay, but as I write, with the poinsettia flinging its scarlet banners over countless walls in the residential district of Asunción, mere history and human triumphs and failures seem unimportant. The Paraguayan poinsettia is a tree rather than the potted plant displayed in American floral shops at Christmas time and, to my unscientific eye, the flapping petals seem much larger than those of our home product. The claims of Paraguay to be known as a land of flowers are strengthened by the gorgeous purple clusters of the Bougainvillea which everywhere arrest and charm the eye."[1]

MEREDITH NICHOLSON, 1934

IN THE YEARS FOLLOWING HIS WIFE'S DEATH, NICHOLSON LIVED in the "upper back rooms" of the University Club, at Meridian and Michigan streets in downtown Indianapolis, with two other bachelor friends, Carleton B. McCulloch and banker Elmer Stout. The author had been forced to give up his North Meridian Street home and was living on rapidly dwindling resources during the early difficult years of the Great Depression. He had no prospects for a job, although he would have jumped at an offer for a place with a newspaper or perhaps a newsmagazine, even ones with late evening deadlines, something he had avoided for most of his years as a reporter or editor.[2]

Fortunately for Nicholson, unlike most others in the unemployment lines, he had friends in high places, and they were exploring every possible avenue in trying to find employment for Nicholson, preferably a position with the government that carried prestige as well as a salary commensurate with his prominence and reputation as an author. Fortunately, too, the Democratic Party was then in power, so his prospects, as a lifelong loyal party member and activist, were good. Not only was Nicholson a close friend of Indiana's newly installed first family, Paul

IHS, BASS PHOTO COMPANY COLLECTION, P130

Indiana governor Paul McNutt greets President Franklin D. Roosevelt during a visit by the president to Indianapolis, circa 1930s.

and Kathleen McNutt, but he was also known, at least by reputation, to the new president, Franklin D. Roosevelt. Moreover, President Roosevelt had personally, and warmly, acknowledged Nicholson's telegram of congratulations upon his election, which also praised Roosevelt's literary style and his political rhetoric. This comment, said the president-elect, was most welcome, for it came from "an expert" and was, "therefore, doubly dear."[3]

Thus, the entreaties made on Nicholson's behalf for a suitable position in the Roosevelt administration fell upon receptive ears, and six months into his first term in 1933, Roosevelt named Nicholson as his personal representative in Paraguay, a country then in the beginning stages of a bitter war with its neighbor Bolivia over the supposedly gas- and oil-rich territory known as the Gran Chaco. Nicholson, who at that time had probably never heard of the Chaco, was pleased to accept the honor and the responsibility of such a significant government position.

Nicholson's first official notice of his possible appointment to a position in Paraguay had come by telegram on August 11, 1933, from Secretary of State Cordell Hull, asking if such an appointment was "acceptable." Nicholson replied at once that it was "entirely satisfactory and greatly appreciated." This set in motion the steps needed to make it happen—a cable to the American legation in Paraguay stating the president's desire to appoint Nicholson as "Envoy Extraordinary and Minister Plenipotentiary of the United States to Paraguay," and asking it to ascertain if this was agreeable to the Paraguayan government, adding that full biographical details for Nicholson were available in the latest edition of *Who's Who in America, 1932–1933*. Upon Paraguay's reply agreeing to the appointment, the State Department invited Nicholson to report for "a period of instruction" of approximately thirty days prior to his departure in early October for South America. His salary was to be $10,000 a year beginning upon the day of his oath of office "which should be taken before you depart for Washington in time to report for duty early in September." His compensation also included travel expenses and a per diem of $5 while traveling, and an application for a diplomatic passport was included.[4]

Things moved rapidly once Nicholson accepted the chance to go to South America. Although the historical records for this period of Nicholson's life are thin, without any letters or comments from the new diplomat or his immediate family, we know that an Indianapolis "Farewell to Nicholson" committee was immediately founded and that it quickly planned an elaborate dinner to honor their friend and give him a memorable send-off to a remote land. The high-level committee, chaired by McCulloch, also included William Fortune, Samuel D. Miller, G. Barrett Moxley, and David Laurence Chambers, and held its initial meeting on August 22, barely two weeks before Nicholson was to leave and the dinner had to be held.

They made many decisions that day—to hold the dinner at the Indianapolis Athletic Club, which limited the number of attendees to four hundred; to make it for men only for reasons of space; and to charge $5 a plate, half going for the dinner and half for other expenses.[5]

The committee also decided to give the guests, as a souvenir of the affair and through the good offices of Bobbs-Merrill executive Chambers, a signed copy of Nicholson's most recent (and last) book, *Old Familiar Faces*, a most appropriate token because of its heavily autobiographical content. Amazingly, all the pieces fell into place on time, and at the "Gala Dinner," held on September 6, 1933, "every [Indianapolis] man of consequence," according to the *Indianapolis Star*, was in attendance. A distinguished array of speakers, headed by another Indiana author, humorist George Ade, were introduced by toastmaster McCulloch, who added his own tribute in the form of the lyrics to "On the Road to Paraguay" and read cablegrams from Hull, whom Nicholson had met while in Tennessee doing research for his Andrew Jackson book; both Indiana senators (Frederick Van Nuys and James Watson); four university presidents; and Yale University professor William Lyons Phelps, editor of the *Letters of James Whitcomb Riley*. McCulloch, in remarks published before the day of the dinner, said it was "difficult to write of Nicholson in terms sufficiently appreciative without making it sound like an obituary," but he went on to say that Nicholson, "in thought, as in deed, is essentially a democrat and I do not mean this in a political sense at all." Instead, McCulloch called Nicholson "a man who loved his fellow man," abhorred snobbery and hypocrisy, was generous to a fault, and "embodied all of chivalry and high-mindedness."[6]

That Nicholson was highly regarded and was expected to make his mark in diplomacy is indicated in the story first announcing his appointment. Everett C. Watkins, writing from Washington, D.C., for the *Indianapolis Star*'s Washington Bureau, suggested that Nicholson's service in Paraguay, a romantic and primitive country mired in a war, offered him the opportunity "to serve as a peacemaker." Under ordinary circumstances, the Paraguayan post would not be as desirable as others in South America, but the "delicate situation there [required] the services of a man with Mr. Nicholson's ability."[7]

Although there is no written record of these developments, it is clear from subsequent events that Nicholson had decided not to make the trip to Paraguay alone, and at some point between the time of his appointment, August 19, and his departure for Washington, D.C., on September 7 to begin monthlong briefings at the State Department, he made a proposal of marriage to his secretary, Dorothy Wolfe Lannon, who had been his employee only briefly. Very little is known about her other than the published report at the time of the wedding in Washington, D.C., literally on the eve of their departure for South America, that she was from Marion, in Grant County, Indiana, and that she was also "a writer."[8]

Since Nicholson had to leave town early in September, he went alone, and Lannon met him in Washington later in the month. Nicholson wrote to Dorothy from the Willard Hotel on September 10 "that how to effect our wedding still puzzles me," but he expected the wife of Senator Van Nuys, "to think of something." Since various foreign ministers were expected to be there, Nicholson did want "some showing of official dignity . . . [to] impress the folks back home." He reminded Dorothy she needed to be there a day or two early to take care of the license and such matters and then closed with the remark, "I'm crazy to see you and have you for keeps. Much love, Meredith."[9]

What Marie Van Nuys thought of was to have the couple marry in the Van Nuys apartment, apparently without any foreign dignitaries or even any family members present. Although Nicholson and the Indiana senator were not close friends, Nicholson had supported his campaign of 1932 and deeply appreciated the senator's assistance. The new couple departed for New York City immediately following the ceremony. More parties lay in store for them there as Nicholson's literary friends, syndicated columnist O. O. McIntyre, *Cosmopolitan* editor Ray Long, and Kentucky humorist Irwin Cobb (whose sister had married Hewitt H. Howland), hosted and toasted the newlyweds. The Nicholsons also attended the premier of Kenyon

Nicholson's new Broadway play, *Sailors Beware*, which Nicholson and the New York critics called a "big success," as was Dorothy. A pleased Nicholson noted she had been "liked by everyone."[10]

Nicholson also told McCulloch that his days were very crowded "with reporters and photographers on [his] trail" and noted that he had two suitcases full of letters and telegrams to be answered. But, he assured his friend, "I'm feelin' sort o' good, ole boy. And the Paraguayans are driving back the Bolivians—captured 3,000 of the birds yesterday." He then thanked McCulloch for "all you did to start me on this adventure" and promised to write again soon, and often.[11]

The Nicholsons sailed from New York City aboard the S.S. *Southern Cross*, a liner that was already sold out, but through a "considerable rearrangement of space," the ship-master was able to provide a large cabin, complete with private bath, for the Nicholsons, and they had a delightful cruise down the Atlantic "in the smoothest of seas" to Buenos Aires, Argentina, stopping only at Rio de Janeiro to accommodate a large number of Brazilians returning from the Chicago World's Fair. The cruise, in effect a honeymoon for the Nicholsons, who had been on the move constantly in recent weeks, was made more pleasant by the captain, who regularly welcomed them to the bridge at night and pointed out the stars and galaxies in the moon-lit sky. The seas roughened near the end of the journey, but they endured it well and arrived at Buenos Aires on October 18. The Nicholsons were flattered to be met on the dock by U.S. ambassador to Argentina Alexander W. Weddle and his wife.[12]

This was the prelude to a delightful four-day stay in that capital city that included cocktail parties and teas hosted by the Weddles and British Ambassador Henry Chilton and his wife. Mrs. Katherine Chilton was an American from Michigan who knew several of Nicholson's former neighbors on Mackinac Island, so their reception in South America was most pleasant. Ambassador Weddle, with whom Nicholson formed an immediate attachment, knew (as Nicholson reported to McCulloch) "all our poets and a lot more, in four languages." Nicholson also reported to McCulloch, a bit enviously, perhaps, for he had arrived in Asunción before writing the letter, that the Weddles lived "in a palace of a house, with service no end, but they are," he concluded, "*great* people and deserve a palace."[13]

Nicholson's remarks at a luncheon in the American Club in Buenos Aires went over well, after which the Nicholsons embarked on the final leg of their journey to Paraguay's capital Asunción, a four-day trip on a steamboat up the Parana and Paraguay rivers. Partway up the estuary at Buenos Aires, the river forked, the right channel leading to Uruguay, the left channel to Asunción. One can imagine how lonely and distant Nicholson must have felt upon his arrival in such a remote place. North American newspapers customarily arrived in Asunción a minimum of four days after publication, radio reception from North America was spotty and often nonexistent, and mail from home, received only once a week, carried letters that had been written twelve or more days before. Even air-mail letters required about a week.[14]

Nicholson's first look at the American minister's home in Asunción must have been disappointing, too. He called it "a queer old shack, most impressive from the front, but bare and bleak within. The ceilings are enormously high, hence the stairway to the bare sleeping room is more alpinish than that at the U[niversity] C[lub]." Moreover, they were told that, "owing to the heat," it was "imperative to sleep on the second floor" of the house.[15]

The Nicholsons, however, adapted well to their new surroundings and got caught up at once in the often "tedious routine" of diplomatic life, which Nicholson enjoyed. His formal duties began with the presentation of his credentials on October 30, 1933, an audience with President Eusebio Ayala and brief comments by Nicholson, in which he promised to do his best "to strengthen the good relations between our countries." Nicholson also assured the president that he possessed a vast curiosity about his country, "which runs so far back into the traditions and achievements of the Western Hemisphere. The State of Indiana, from which I come, in the United States of America, seems very youthful in comparison." A few

days later, when Nicholson was honored at a reception by
the Pan American Cultural Society, Nicholson reported an
unusual "display of warmth" and his belief "that anti-Amer-
ican feelings in Paraguay are not by any means general."
When Doctor V. Galeano responded for the Paraguayans,
he praised the new American minister's "splendid record"
as an author and said that Paraguay needed "such worthy
diplomatic representatives" during its "trying period" of
the war, which was producing "international anarchy."[16]

The Nicholsons were also welcomed to Asunción by
the American Society of Paraguay, a sizable group that
included many faculty members of the Colegio International, a school operated by the United Christian Mission-
ary Society headquartered in Indianapolis. At the dinner
given for them, Doctor Arthur E. Elliott, president of the
college, made a long opening speech identifying Nicholson
to the group "as the dean of American men of letters" and
as one with "many qualities which fit him admirably for his
present important position." Elliott's remarks, reprinted
in full in the *Indianapolis Star*, ended with the thought
that Nicholson was "the most distinguished American
that has ever represented the United States of America
in this republic," and, quoting Ade's remark at Nicholson's
farewell dinner in Indianapolis, Elliott gave the newest
interpretation of one of the New Deal's most prominent
"alphabet" administrations: the NRA really "means 'Nicholson, Reliable, Always.'"[17]

Happily, after helping launch Nicholson's diplomatic career, McCulloch continued to do good things for Nicholson, particularly through the marvelously witty and erudite letters he regularly sent to him. More than anyone else, McCulloch kept Nicholson in touch with what was happening in his beloved Indiana even though he was thousands of miles away. And Nicholson responded in kind by keeping McCulloch in touch, as fully as possible given security considerations, with his activities in Asunción.

Of course, these activities were dominated by the Chaco War, which intensified in 1933, just prior to Nicholson's arrival in the capital city, and continued into 1935, just after Nicholson transferred to a new post. But Nicholson did play an important role in its conduct through the instant rapport and friendship he developed with President Ayala, an outstanding humanist and scholar but perhaps a bit naïve as a politician. Yet he has been called "the best president Paraguay ever had," and other scholars have noted that he had written articles on education and literature.[18]

The conflict between Paraguay and Bolivia over the territory known as the Chaco Boreal was the bitterest "inter-American dispute" of the century, according to American diplomat Sumner Wells. The area was large, some 150,000 square miles, roughly the size of Montana (and four times the size of Indiana), but it was economically marginal, "without vegetable or mineral wealth."

Rumors persisted, however, that there were valuable petroleum deposits in the Chaco, and that American "dollar diplomacy" or "petroleum imperialism," specifically the Standard Oil Company, backed Bolivia's attempted military takeover of the low-lying territory. Repeatedly, League of Nations commissioners tried to mediate the dispute, but these efforts, apart from an armistice perhaps foolishly suggested by Ayala in late December 1933, came to nothing (other than a chance for Bolivia to bolster its fighting prowess during it). Fighting resumed in January when the truce expired, but eventually an agreement on June 12, 1935, ended the hostilities, and a peace treaty followed in 1938. By then, however, Ayala had been replaced, ending thirty-two years of "liberal rule" in Paraguay.[19]

Over the course of his service in Asunción, Nicholson submitted regular monthly reports on the "General Conditions Prevailing in Paraguay." The Bolivian war dominated the "political relations" section of these reports, which contained careful summaries of relevant local press commentary, public communications from neighboring countries, and the official Paraguayan response to them. In the concluding "Miscellaneous" category, Nicholson's flair for interesting writing and astute political insights is displayed as is his knowledge of local actions and attitudes. His newspaper background also helped him in preparing these reports and other dispatches. His first report, which covered events during October 1933, also pointed to alarming "health conditions in Asunción," exacerbated by the absence of a sewer system.[20]

The next report in January 1934, delayed by the "pressure of other work," covered the final two months of 1933 and opened with remarks about the Paraguayans still believing that American money, either through the Standard Oil Company or other sources, was aiding Bolivia in the Chaco. Nicholson also provided detailed information regarding the war and Paraguay's "much improved" military position following a new offensive early in December against "demoralized" Bolivian soldiers, after which another armistice went into effect. During the armistice Ayala expected the League of Nations to arrange for a meeting "in a neutral country" of plenipotentiaries from the belligerent nations.[21] Part of the reason for lack of energy among Bolivia's much larger army was that most of their soldiers were Indians from the *altiplano*, or extremely high elevation (twelve thousand feet) in La Paz, and found conditions in the low-lying, insect- and snake-infested swamplands of the Chaco dispiriting.

Nicholson's January report, written shortly after the truce ended, highlighted the renewed hostility toward the United States in the Paraguayan press and the revived charge that the Standard Oil Company had made Bolivia its "fief." Moreover, since Paraguay now clearly had the upper hand in the war, "mediation was unwanted and resented," and Paraguayans were insisting that they keep the fruits of their hard-earned victories. But attitudes softened and public opinion regarding America improved although the arbitration efforts of Buenos Aires had "failed absolutely." In a confidential section of this report, however, Nicholson indicated that the war was not going quite as well as public reports stated, and that the Bolivian Air Force was inflicting heavy damages on Paraguay, "virtually defenseless against air attacks."[22]

These reports also covered movements of personnel in all the other embassies in Asunción and some occasional historic references. Nicholson once pointed out, for example, that between 1912 and 1928, when there should have been four administrations of four years' duration each, that there were eight presidents, four vice presidents, and fifty-nine cabinet members. These seventy-one offices, however, were held by only twenty-eight men who shifted about. "The tendency here," he wrote, "is for the government to be like a monopoly held by a few families." He also noted in his June 1934 letter that there was increasing dissatisfaction with the Ayala regime and that "popular unrest is growing." Moreover, the cost of living was up, speculation was rampant, and the proposed draft of ten thousand men was resented by the working classes; overall, the war was imposing severe strains both upon the government and the economy of Paraguay.[23]

Nevertheless, as Nicholson stated in an article he wrote for a diplomatic journal, Paraguay was one of the "most interesting and picturesque countries in South America." Unfortunate in its history in that the War of the Pacific, 1865–70, almost literally decimated the country's population, a loss that required fully six decades to overcome, Paraguay in the 1930s nonetheless exhibited Old World charm and a slow, unhurried way of life in its capital city. The country was also known for its lace, its music, and its beautiful countryside. Bridle paths in the vicinity of Asunción bore a romantic appearance; "when the famous flowering trees with their gorgeous purples, rich yellows, flaming reds, and delicate orchids are in bloom," enthused Nicholson, the Arcadian scene "is unequalled anywhere."[24]

Yet a North American would find some things unsettling. As Nicholson had quickly learned, there were "flies and skeeters" everywhere; the city had no water supply and no sewer system; the homes had no fireplaces or furnaces, even though temperatures dipped to near freezing at times; and the streets were unpaved and often precipitous. Nicholson even remarked upon these conditions in his first report back to the State Department, reporting that in Asunción, "a city of about 100,000 population ... waste water is freely discharged into the streets. Flies abound. Mosquitoes are plentiful." And he worried about the "alarming increase in infant mortality from intestinal diseases both in Asunción and the rural districts" and the unsanitary conditions in and around crowded military hospitals in the city's business center.[25]

Initially, McCulloch had jokingly stated that he hoped the war would not end before Nicholson arrived so that he could be the peacemaker and then "get decorated by both countries with the 'Order of the Condor, First Class,'" but he need not have worried. The war outlasted Nicholson's stay by a few months, but not before he had established himself as an excellent representative of his country. Ayala regularly had fellow author Nicholson as a dinner guest, an honor accorded no other member of the small diplomatic corps there, which included representatives from Germany, Italy, Spain, and a number of neighboring South American countries. During their dinner discussions, Ayala often shared with Nicholson advance information about military moves or peacemaking initiatives, which Nicholson in turn shared with his superiors in Washington, putting him, as he confided to McCulloch, about "ten laps ahead of the other dips [*sic*]" and, in the process, making him so valuable to the United States that his desires, after a year in Paraguay, for a transfer could not be granted at once. But Nicholson made the best of it, doing his duty manfully while trying to learn the language, something Dorothy also undertook quite successfully, in time even managing casual conversations with the locals, the domestic help, and others.[26]

For his part, McCulloch kept Nicholson informed of political activities at home, which proved to be of considerable interest to the diplomat, and also made a regular necrology report as many of their mutual friends passed on with alarming regularity. He also kept Nicholson up on his own and Elmer and "Pop's" (Oscar Welborn) social activities, if any. Once in October, perhaps to taunt Nicholson about his season-reversed location and his hot weather then, he said it's "cold here, as cold as a pawnbroker's eye" (quoting a Riley line), but overall his comments kept Nicholson fully informed of the remarkable achievements of "Paul," as the governor, Paul V. McNutt, delivered on his promises for an improved economy, a reformed state government, and an efficient welfare and relief program. McCulloch campaigned with McNutt in the 1934 off-year elections, which included all the seats in the state and national House of Representatives and half the seats in the Indiana Senate, and kept Nicholson advised of developments there. The Democratic margin over the Republicans in the House of Representatives was an unbelievable 91 to 9 as a result of the 1932 elections, and that number decreased but slightly in 1934. McCulloch said that McNutt, during a New York trip, was "making about two speeches a day, including Syracuse University, the New York Times staff, etc. He'll be president someday if he doesn't hit his knee."[27]

While still state Democratic chairman and campaigning with McNutt, their "barnstorming" took them to

"Delphi, Crawfordsville, Bedford, Vincennes, Newcastle, Marion, South Bend, Winamac and other important centers," McCulloch assured Nicholson that McNutt "certainly makes a wonderful speech," and then repeated his prediction: "I think he is headed for the White House." Some months earlier, when they were in Washington together while driving past the White House, McCulloch reached over and grabbed McNutt's wrist to check his pulse rate and then pointed to the mansion but, he reported, there was "no increase."[28]

Probably of greatest interest to Nicholson, however, were McCulloch's reports on the promising start of a political career by Nicholson's daughter-in-law, whose campaign for the Indiana General Assembly began in 1934. Indeed, McCulloch took the credit for getting Roberta West Nicholson to consider running for a seat in the state legislature, saying that her goal, at first, had been to follow in her father-in-law's steps and run for a seat on the city council. But she accepted McCulloch's advice to look higher, and her successful run made her the only female member of the Indiana House of Representatives in 1935–37. Her social activism there quickly, as McCulloch proudly reported, made her "famous throughout the land." A firm believer in equal rights for women, Nicholson had introduced and pushed to passage an anti-alimony bill, known in the press as the "heart-balm" bill. As explained by McCulloch, Roberta had filed a bill "prohibiting the filing of suits for alienation of affection or seduction and prohibiting the naming of correspondents. Inasmuch as it was introduced by a woman, all the men voted for it. Only seven were in opposition. It passed the House. It now goes before the Senate and will, they say, be passed with equal enthusiasm. There is no close organization of Gold Diggers to fight it, and responsible women cannot oppose it without being misunderstood. It looks as if our sex is finally going to be protected." Indeed, many other states promptly adopted similar legislation, some laws being exact copies of the Nicholson original.[29] As McCulloch further reported in 1935, "the *Chicago Tribune* carried an editorial on her [Roberta]. The *New York Times* and, in fact, papers all over the country have commented on it [the heart-balm bill] and given her full recognition for it. For a day or two, they spoke of her as Mrs. Meredith Nicholson, Jr., daughter-in-law of the distinguished author who is now Minister to Paraguay but after the first two or three days, she went ahead under her own power and now is spoken of as 'Mrs. Roberta West Nicholson.'"[30]

While these exciting developments were continuing in Indiana, there were also exciting times much farther south for the Nicholsons. Tall, dignified, even stern-looking when appropriate, Nicholson appeared very much the model of his genre and got along well with his fellow "dips," as he called them privately, but he also termed the diplomatic corps a "vast whispering gallery." Nicholson, by nature quite gregarious, could also be cordial and congenial, even garrulous, in his informal moments. Surprisingly, because of the high turnover rate among them, Nicholson became "Dean of the Diplomatic Corps" in Asunción in August 1934, which led to a few additional responsibilities. His main problem, however, revealed to others only after he had solved it, was dealing with a deceitful secretary of the legation, one Robert Jarvis, whom Nicholson described as the "most awful ass I have ever known. Pompous, conceited, condescending, tricky, disloyal. I suffered him for four months and nearly got nervous prostration for my tolerance." That young foreign service officer "had never been on the diplomatic side before, having been in the consular service, mostly in India. His promotion went to his head." Moreover, on the personal side, Jarvis was "terribly, most offensively Briticized, aided in this expatriation by an Anglo-Indian wife. They both quite frankly expressed their contempt for everything U.S.A." Warming to his rant on the pair, Nicholson went on to say that "it would take a book to give you an idea of their assinity [*sic*]. He [Jarvis] wouldn't think I could do anything here until he had rushed to the British Legation to consult the chargé there. Our business here is, not negligibly, to make friends for the U.S. and it seemed rather poor patriotism to run this chancellery as an outpost of King George's dominions."[31]

Nicholson went on to tell his Indiana confidant that the last straw was when Jarvis, who pried into Nicholson's private dispatches with the State Department, went to the British Legation with a special message that had been given to Nicholson by President Ayala for transmission to Secretary of State Hull, then in Montevideo, Uruguay, at the Pan American conference. But "the stupid Secretary at the British Legation let it out to me the next day that Jarvis had told the chargé of this." Accordingly, Nicholson said, "I had taken about all my nerves would stand from the Jarvises." So he sent a short note to Hull, then with the Weddles in Buenos Aires, seeking some redress, and "within 48 hours [came] a cable transferring J. to Antofagasta, Chile as counsel—putting him quite out of the dip. service." This, of course, created quite a stir within the American offices in Asunción—"he [Jarvis] crawled, he begged, he would do anything if I would ask for a revocation of the order, —said I had ruined his career." But Nicholson stood his ground: "I told the cowardly skunk he had done all he could to ruin mine and he could go plum to _____ [*sic*] Antofagasta, the least desirable spot on all the continent. The furious protests he cabled to the Department made the Atlantic boil, but they were not answered to him at all." Instead, Jarvis was ordered to proceed at once to his new assignment, and Nicholson was satisfied, feeling like he had removed "a deceased cat from under the porch." It was, he believed, "such asses as J. who say 'clark' and 'immejut' and 'shedule' who cause wild west congressmen to take a shot at foreign service boys—the career men. I'm for a trained diplomatic service, but it ought to be <u>Ameri-can</u>." Nicholson was then doubly pleased because his new secretary, Henry W. Butler, was "a highly capable young man," an engineering graduate of the University of Illinois who had formerly served in the Chilean embassy and on the Mexican border in the U.S. Army and elsewhere, and was "a peach of a fellow." He concluded, "We Thank God—& the Department—every hour for the Butlers." Butler's wife was also very accomplished as a linguist, a talent much admired by Nicholson.[32]

In addition to his frank and open correspondence with McCulloch, Nicholson also had frequent contacts with David L. Chambers. Not surprisingly, these letters often referred to writing projects. It appears that Nicholson had a novel under way at the time his South American adventures started but nothing further is known about the work Chambers referred to as "Almost Annie," or whether it ever got beyond the working title. Nicholson always denied that he wanted to do a South American novel or write about Paraguay. First of all, it was "against the rules" of the State Department for him to write about the country to which he was accredited and secondly, the living conditions—unbearable heat, as high as 115 degrees Fahrenheit, in the summer and nippy days in the winter, in unheated houses "except for small electric heaters about the size of a watch"—made additional literary endeavors impossible. Twice in the same letter to McCulloch, Nicholson used an emphatic he seldom employed and said it was "damned hot," and later during the month, more subtly, he informed Chambers that it was "hotter nell."[33]

Among Nicholson's deferred plans for writing projects were a "book of letters," a novel told through the correspondence of its protagonists—something Dorothy had suggested; another play with Kenyon Nicholson (subject unknown); and, possibly, another historical novel on the life of an interesting American, like the one he had done on Andrew Jackson, but he never followed through on any of these ideas. He told Chambers he once dreamed about a great idea for a novel but could not recapture it when he was awake. He also unburdened himself to Chambers, saying that he should never have tried to do "realistic" works. Instead, the real Nicholson was in his *House of a Thousand Candles* and *Madness of May* books.

Nicholson's longstanding desire for a transfer from Paraguay was quickened by his knowledge of openings in Albania, an Adriatic Sea location that was strongly appealing, and in the Irish Free State, where Nicholson believed that his knowledge of Irish lore, aided by his Irish ancestry, would give him an advantage, but these hopes went unfulfilled. Not only did Roosevelt want to keep Nicholson in South America and draw upon his special access to information, but upon closer examination Nicholson realized he could not afford the more glamorous, and more expensive, European posts. As it was, he said, only through the favorable rates of exchange that Americans enjoyed in Paraguay was he able to meet his expenses. All "entertainments," of which many were required in order to keep pace with other legations at which wine and cocktails were ever present, were paid for, largely, by the minister personally. Even Nicholson's requests for a new staff member, a translator, went unanswered except for the suggestion that the legation use the exchange rate benefits for that person.

Eventually, long after the president had relented and agreed to Nicholson's transfer in 1934, it could not be made effective until February 1935. In the meantime, Nicholson received permission for a short "regular leave," not a "home leave," after more than a year at work in Asunción. This enabled the Nicholsons to revisit Buenos Aires in December, where they enjoyed life in a more congenial urban setting and Nicholson substituted for Ambassador Weddle and delivered a major speech to the American Club. He chose American humor as his topic and reported to McCulloch, again using a line from Riley, one of the American humorists he had discussed, "there wasn't a dry aisle in the place" when he finished. The talk, duly reported in the Argentine press as well as in the Buenos Aires delegation's regular dispatch to Washington, was a great success, as were previous short-notice talks Nicholson had given to South American audiences on the meanings and traditions of Memorial Day and Thanksgiving Day in the United States.[34]

Overall, it can be concluded that Nicholson did a commendable job as a neophyte diplomat, and that, despite occasional discomforts, he found the experience rather pleasant. Happily for the Nicholsons, shortly after returning to their upriver home from Buenos Aires, they learned of his appointment to the American Legation in Caracas, Venezuela. This was a city McCulloch had visited in 1913, and he told Nicholson it was "a little Paris," much closer to home than Paraguay. Its location on the itinerary of several Caribbean cruise ships meant there would most likely be a number of Indiana friends able to call on them there (and undoubtedly "increase your living expenses as well").[35] Nevertheless, it was with a quickened footstep that Nicholson took leave of Asunción after bidding a fond farewell to Ayala and headed back to the United States. Following an extensive debriefing in Washington, the Nicholsons returned to Indianapolis for the first time as a married couple.

10

Broken Barriers

*"The world is a different place every morning; but that's only
an old habit the world has. It keeps spinning a little faster all
the time. . . . Everybody is restless; people are living as though they
expected to die tomorrow and are afraid they're going
to miss something; but I don't believe people are wickeder than
they used to be. What we used to call wicked we call naughty now,
and pretend it doesn't matter!"*[1]

MEREDITH NICHOLSON, 1922

MEREDITH AND DOROTHY NICHOLSON VERY MUCH ENJOYED
their brief return to the United States early in 1935,
which was highlighted by a quick visit to Indianapolis and
included parties given by family and friends. Especially
memorable was the dinner that Nicholson's closest friends,
Carleton B. McCulloch and Elmer Stout, personally had
prepared for their former housing companion, and overall
the leave time flew by quickly. After more "instruction" for
the new minister to Venezuela in March and April, the Nicholsons arrived in Caracas in mid-April, and Nicholson for-
mally took charge of the legation there on April 22, 1935.

The couple had looked forward eagerly to this post-
ing at a bright spot in Latin America, about which they
had heard many good things. Mary Lou Weddle, wife
of the American ambassador in Buenos Aires, assured

Dorothy, just before the Nicholsons left a still quite primitive Paraguay, that they would like their new situation
because "Everyone speaks so highly of Caracas—[it] has
a nice climate, and the 'colony' there has always had the
name of being gay."[2] Similarly, in the story that accompanied a photograph of the U.S. Minister's residence in
Caracas, the Nicholsons' new home, the reporter called
the city one of "the show places of South America."[3]

But the country was also a dictatorship—its *caudillo*,
with absolute control over the country's military and eco-
nomic might, was the semiliterate Juan Vicente Gomez.
President Gomez had seized power in 1908, when his
predecessor was out of the country, and he gradually and
ruthlessly improved the country's and his own wealth and
influence. A major factor had been the discovery of oil in
the Lake Maricaibo basin in 1918, the profits of which
Gomez used to build roads and a few schools and otherwise develop an infrastructure without doing much for the
citizens of his country, who were kept in control through
brutal repression. According to John Gunther, who visited Venezuela shortly after the Nicholsons lived there,
under Gomez there had been literally thousands of political prisoners, "who dragged out their lives bearing leg
irons (*grillos*) that made them permanent cripples," and
that there were dozens more who had been cruelly tor-
tured and executed. Hubert Herring confirms this point
in his magisterial survey of the country's history, calling

the "tortures reminiscent of the Dark Ages." Yet he also pointed out that Gomez was "skillful in public administration," and that he had eliminated Venezuela's foreign debt, made many public improvements, and "maintained good relations with foreign powers." In the process, he also became, reputedly, "the richest man in South America," leaving an estate estimated at $200 million.[4]

In the course of these developments, Gomez built for himself a lavish one-hundred-room palace at Maracay, near Caracas, and, although he never married, became the proud father of perhaps as many as a hundred children, most of whom carried the Gomez name and received offices and endowments from their father. Personable and an admirer of the United States, Gomez also liked the new minister, and Nicholson occasionally visited the president at his country home.

Nicholson quickly settled into his new job, one that he came to enjoy enormously while also regretting that his duties precluded time for writing anything substantial. He was even hard-pressed to get off what was usually a weekly letter to "Carlo" McCulloch, such letters being dashed off in pencil (to write in ink would take twice as long, Nicholson claimed) on "mail day," usually a Saturday when the legation's diplomatic pouch would be sent, by air, to the United States. Nevertheless, McCulloch very much appreciated these interesting missives, which he took pleasure in sharing with a few of Nicholson's friends.

Nicholson particularly enjoyed being close enough to the United States to hear radio newscasts, even WLW in Cincinnati; receive its newspapers in a timely fashion; and otherwise be able to stay in touch with events in the states, particularly his home state. He also relished occasional visits of friends from Indiana and elsewhere, including such well-known figures as the Rockefellers (checking up, perhaps, on their oil company's production), Mary Roberts Rinehart, and Amelia Earhart. Visitors from Indiana included the Lilly brothers, J. K. and Eli; daughter Elizabeth and her husband, Austin H. Brown; and others, usually prominent doctors and lawyers known to the Nicholsons. Contrary to a published report, the visitors did not include his son Meredith Jr., and his wife, Roberta (for reasons of the expense and little desire on their part to spend any time with the new Mrs. Nicholson), nor could Nicholson ever persuade McCulloch and Stout to make the trip. Had they come, they would have seen many familiar sights in Nicholson's home and office, where he had at least four photographs of James Whitcomb Riley and signed ones of Booth Tarkington, George Ade, and John T. McCutcheon. The only non-Hoosier to be included was Professor George Edward Woodberry, the man Nicholson credited with getting him started as a writer. Nicholson also told McCulloch that Riley was mentioned in the legation at least once every day, and that he and others frequently quoted favorite lines of his poetry. Nicholson's close friendship with McCulloch continued through a correspondence that is remarkably full, candid, and witty; these exchanges between Nicholson and McCulloch (few others seem to have survived) provide an insight into the social and political history of Indiana and Indianapolis in the 1930s, and their occasional reminiscences about events of long ago serve to underscore Nicholson's comment that all history cannot be found between the covers of a book.

In May 1935 the Nicholsons made a delightful automobile trip to the Caribbean coast, took a few dips in the blue waters, and soon thereafter visited Gomez at his estate at Maracay, as well as one of his "vast coffee plantations." McCulloch liked to tease Nicholson about the president and his many children, saying upon viewing a picture of the aged man he failed to detect "what there was about him that has such a virile appeal that all his wives and concubines should have presented him with over one hundred pledges of their affection," and wondered if Nicholson had already memorized the names of all the offspring. Nicholson ignored such gibes, and continued in the good graces of the powerful man and his country. On July 4, 1935, the Nicholsons hosted a large reception for approximately 350 guests, which was followed, of course, by many more "feedings" and "cocktailings," practices which seem to have led to excesses by both Nicholson and his wife. "We continue to like Caracas," Nicholson stated. "There are people here who measure up with any I ever knew of anywheres" [*sic*].

Another elaborate festivity was the Thanksgiving Day dinner the Nicholsons gave for fourteen staff members (and two "ringers") at their home. Following morning church services, in which Nicholson solemnly read President Franklin D. Roosevelt's Thanksgiving proclamation "in a sonorous voice [that was] much admired," the minister and his wife served two North American turkeys (the Latin American variety being very poor) with all the trimmings, including applause-getting "punkin pie." They even presided over a second dinner of imported lamb for other guests, and Nicholson credited his wife for the great meals produced. "She works on a dinner," he stated, "as if it were a sonnet or a rondeau," with results that were spectacular and very well received.[5]

The Nicholsons' plans for spending Christmas at home in 1935 were spoiled by the death of the aged Gomez in December of that year. Consequently, Nicholson remained in Caracas, and although the record is unclear, it appears that Dorothy made the trip alone and spent part of the holidays with her adopted family. The Nicholson family, however, did not warm to Dorothy, and she did herself no favors while trying to overcome their latent hostility by "overindulging" on perhaps more than one occasion, even to the point of sickness in one of the children's homes. These missteps continued in 1937, when Dorothy visited Indianapolis alone and again embarrassed herself and onlookers by trying to light a kitchen match, which she thought was a cigarette, with a candle. (When an amused Charles Nicholson called brother Med Jr., who was away on a business trip at the time, to tell him of Dorothy's latest faux pas, Med said he hoped she had burned her nose!)[6] Some of the hard feelings towards her undoubtedly stemmed from loyalty to Eugenie Nicholson, still acutely missed and most fondly remembered. Called by her daughter-in-law the "most wonderful woman I ever knew," Eugenie had established a difficult standard for Dorothy to meet. To some extent, of course, Dorothy reciprocated with coolness to the other Nicholsons, as even Meredith recognized. He wrote to Dorothy in 1940, while she was in California recuperating from a nervous breakdown, that the children "really appreciate you and all you have done for me, more than you know," and he added that "I hope your feeling about them will be more amiable."[7]

As it happened, and perhaps fortunately, there were few occasions for more than brief family visits or get-togethers in Indianapolis during the marriage that lasted just over ten years, and there was only one instance when family members (Austin H. and Elizabeth Brown) called upon the Nicholsons in any of their three Latin American postings. But until their separation in 1943, Nicholson remained loyal and devoted to Dorothy, and he constantly sang her praises to all as an indispensable helpmate in his diplomatic work, some of which was indeed quite strenuous and demanding. In general, life was good, the social scene sparkled, and the Nicholsons enjoyed themselves.

During his wife's absence at the end of 1935, Nicholson participated in the funeral ceremonies for President Gomez. Although Nicholson had just observed his sixty-ninth birthday, the American minister, in formal evening dress, "white tie and topper," dutifully "marched those three awful miles at Maracay behind the remains of King Gomez," but he "resolved never again to give [such] outward and visible signs of being an ass." The British legation, at about the same time, was memorializing the death of King George V, and Nicholson informed his staff that they all would attend in "cutaways, as for a morning wedding."[8]

Having remained in Caracas also meant that Nicholson was on hand to observe the aftermath of Gomez's departure, reported in the North American press as wild rioting and attempts to overthrow the new government. Nicholson instead said the crowds were merely celebrating the end of an era. As he told fellow Hoosier diplomat Claude Bowers in Spain, "the disturbances here when Gomez wrapt the draperies etc. were really in the nature of jubilation at his departure and not a protest against the elevation of General Lopez Contreras into the presidency." Nicholson added that just the other day "a group of new dealers took a large assortment of torture implements from the local prisons down to the sea and flung them to the sharks. A Venezuelan poet read an ode appropriate to the occasion. The transition from the old to the new order has been effected with much less violence than we expected." In the meantime, "the Gomez tribe (somewhat large and without benefit of clergy) and a horde of parasites and grafters have fled, while others, many former exiles, have come home." Nicholson once, perhaps unwisely, rode in his car through the streets during the excitement. No violence occurred, but his car suffered repeated flat tires from the nails and tacks that had been scattered about. As he recognized, the joke was on him because the repairs were at his own expense.[9]

Despite the upset in Caracas at this time, Nicholson was able to find the time to contribute, as requested by Indianapolis reporter William Herschell, an essay reflecting upon Indianapolis history at the time of the centennial of its incorporation. In the charming personal reminiscence, Nicholson discussed having grown up within the city he had moved to when only five years old and recalled many of the city's most interesting people, newspapermen, ministers, and politicians (including the governors from the 1870s on), without recourse to any reference books. Also, in commenting about the Indianapolis bar and bench, he reviewed one of the most famous criminal trials in the city (one he had covered as a reporter), the previously mentioned Simeon Coy trial for tampering with the ballots in the election of 1884. McCulloch soon afterward told Nicholson that his essay received much favorable comment, and his friend Margaret Shipp also complimented Nicholson upon this effort. Nicholson told her he regretted not being able to say more and then he gave the lady a good report on recent events in Caracas.[10]

Much of Nicholson's correspondence in 1936 also dealt with the upcoming American election, about which he had definite opinions and regretted that his participation in it was "by check, not voice," but he wished fervently for the reelection of the president, saying that "his loss would be a loss for all humanity," and that he personally longed to go on the stump and lash out at the perfidy of the "Wall Street" Republicans.[11]

As if stimulated by the recall of his hometown history, Nicholson soon afterward told his Bobbs-Merrill editor, David L. Chambers, that "I fairly reek with good stuff [for a new novel] if only I had time to get it into script." He spoke again of his writing plans during an interview while home on leave in December 1936. He repeated that he had no books under way or planned, but pointed out that he liked to write essays and that he might do that again.[12] (This was exactly what happened, for he spent some of his time in retirement in Indianapolis in the mid-1940s as a columnist for the *Indianapolis Star*.)

In the meantime, Nicholson's tenure as minister in Venezuela continued to go well, even though the cost of

ASSOCIATED PRESS

Nicholson, U.S. minister to Venezuela, is shown in his suite in a hotel in New York, December 4, 1936, as he was interviewed by reporters upon his return to the United States after a two-year absence. Nicholson said that President Roosevelt's Good Neighbor policy was having "the greatest favorable reaction throughout South America."

living in Caracas was "altitudinous" and his entertaining expenses absolutely "appalling." Still, Nicholson seemed to prefer keeping busy, "both socially and officially," and the State Department received a number of spontaneous "commendations" about the good work of its minister in Caracas, including one from an executive of the Standard Oil Company who appreciated Nicholson's assistance to the company.[13]

There was one particularly distressing episode, however, involving embassy personnel, when a plane carrying two Americans and two Latin Americans crashed in a remote, swampy section of the country. The two Latin Americans survived the crash and walked/waded to safety, but both Americans, more seriously injured initially, perished on the site. One, the personable Frederick Grab, Nicholson's commercial attaché, left behind a wife and two small children, and Nicholson was unable to do much to help them afterwards. As he had lamented to McCulloch in an earlier crisis in Paraguay, "I'm too damned emotional," and he found such losses within the diplomatic family very difficult to bear. Particularly upsetting was the long delay before the plane wreckage and the two bodies were found, some seventeen days after the crash, but Nicholson did take part in a memorial service for the two men held in a Caracas church. As described in the local newspaper, Nicholson's participation included reading a portion of a Tennyson ode on death.[14]

There was, however, as Nicholson emphasized to his confidant in Indianapolis, real work to be done by his office. "Some people mistakenly think that all we do is lie around and go to parties, all at government expense, whereas in truth the minister must pay for most of the entertainment from his own pocket," he wrote McCulloch. Nicholson also let off steam privately about inconsiderate and boorish American tourists, who looked upon the legation primarily as a "lunch counter and a comfort station." Indeed, once after spending nearly a full day in delicate negotiations with the local police in order to prevent the arrest of an overly boisterous visitor, the reveler left town without thanking Nicholson for his assistance.[15]

Suddenly, in February 1938 Nicholson received word of his pending transfer to another post. The first intimation of such a move was the news that the baggage and other effects of a successor were being shipped to Caracas. When Nicholson asked the State Department for an explanation, there was no immediate reply, but after a week of waiting, a cable from Secretary of State Cordell Hull came, saying that "The President has asked me to send you this personal message. Owing to exigencies in the Foreign Service, the President has found it necessary to determine upon certain transfers and new appointments." As a result, "he desires to transfer you to from your present post to be Minister in Nicaragua."[16]

Beneath this calm exterior, however, things were happening at a frantic pace back in Washington. There is no written record of what had transpired to cause Nicholson's dismissal from Venezuela, but rumors were rife, and as Roosevelt told his secretary, "I want to see the Secretary of State again about Meredith Nicholson—there are real difficulties there which cannot be a part of the record." Evidently, however, based upon the oral tradition, Dorothy, perhaps in another episode of overindulgence, had been, in the words of Allegra Stewart, "flagrantly indiscreet" (no details given) with some American navy officers to the point that she and her husband would have to leave the legation in Caracas. No explanation was ever made in the official records, newspapers, or even the private correspondence of those knowledgeable. Instead, in a highly unusual step, Hull sent Wayne Coy, a young Indiana bureaucrat then working in Washington, D.C., who knew some of Nicholson's children, to Indianapolis to explain to the family the real reason for the transfer. Roberta West Nicholson accompanied her husband to this highly confidential meeting in Coy's hotel room at the Indianapolis Athletic Club, where he made the explanation. Roberta, the only survivor from this meeting after 1968, eventually spoke about it to friends, but during a recorded interview in 1983, when this subject came up, she asked that the tape recorder be stopped, so still nothing remains in the written record.[17]

The family tradition, however, is that Dorothy's "indis-
cretions" were the cause for the transfer to Nicaragua,
although Nicholson himself seemed totally oblivious to
such actions by his wife and any role she might have played
in the "demotion." His own understanding was that the
move was entirely political; that his successor, Antonio C.
Gonzalez, wanted the Caracas position and was able to get
it. Nicholson never changed his story regarding this matter and remained devoted to his wife throughout her illness, a nervous breakdown suffered in 1940; her recovery
at a sanitarium in California; and indeed throughout their
joint service abroad, after which the couple returned to
Indianapolis. The causes for their eventual estrangement
after living for a short time in Saint Augustine, Florida,
which led to a divorce in 1943, are not known, either.

During a busy return to Washington, D.C., in May
1938, the Nicholsons were also able to squeeze in a perhaps tension-packed short visit to Indianapolis. On the
other hand, Nicholson had a "most cordial" reception at
the White House, where he was able to answer the president's probing questions about matters in South America,
after which he exulted to McCulloch, Roosevelt is "certainly wonderful. The hope of the world indeed."[18]

The Nicholsons arrived in Nicaragua in June 1938 at
a very significant time in the history of the country, just
as they had in Paraguay and Venezuela. In Nicaragua the
Somoza dictatorship, which followed two decades of occu-

pation by the U.S Marine Corps, had just gotten under way and was to last until 1979. Anastasio Somoza, the head of the Nicaragua National Guard, had used his position to seize control of the government in 1937, and Nicholson was on hand to participate in formal inaugural ceremonies in 1938.

Somoza (1896–1956) was educated in the United States, spoke fluent English, and was an engaging conversationalist. Called by John Gunther the "cleverest politician between the Rio Grande and the Panama Canal," Somoza also was courageous, "being the only head of a Central American state who dared leave his own country during his term of office."[19] In Nicholson's view Nicaragua was "a most interesting place." Again they were dismayed with the run-down condition of their new living quarters. Although fairly new (rebuilt following an earthquake in 1931), the "ready-to-wear" bungalow was "precariously situated" on a hillside, the roof leaked, and "the ceiling in the master bedroom may fall according to the Newtonian law without waiting for an earthquake." "It's sad," Nicholson continued, "that our government has not provided decent housing for its representatives." On the bright side, however, Nicholson got along remarkably well with Somoza, who spoke English "in quite the American style" and with whom he shared a great admiration for Roosevelt. Moreover, at their first meeting, Somoza "spoke of my yarn, 'The Little Brown Jug' and what the governor of North Carolina said to the governor of South Carolina, and then laughed heartily." Obviously, this warmed Nicholson to the man, whom he later called a "good fellow in Wabash Valley terms," someone you would like to spend an evening with drinking, playing cards, and swapping tales.[20]

The good feelings were mutual, and Somoza credited Nicholson with giving real meaning to the Roosevelt administration's Good Neighbor policy, which emphasized diplomacy and trade over military force in Central and South America. Indeed, upon Nicholson's eventual departure from Nicaragua, a Managua newspaper praised Nicholson's work in "promoting good will and understanding between the people of North America and Central America." The paper then proposed that Nicaragua establish a special award named for the late Rubén Darío, Nicaragua's foremost poet and author, so that it could be presented to Nicholson. He deserved it because of "his singular action as representative of President Roosevelt, and by the vigor of his personality and the indispensable wit of his exemplary diplomatic career." Nicholson did not receive the award, but did receive an exquisite statue of the country's most famous volcano amid an "unusually warm" farewell ceremony.[21]

But gradually Nicholson was slowing down. He told McCulloch in 1939 that he and Dorothy were often tired, and on August 12, 1939, he admitted to being "very, very tired. Never so busy in my life." Moreover, Nicholson confided to McCulloch that Dorothy had been "miserable" nearly all the time in Nicaragua. This comment came shortly before a "home leave," when the Nicholsons planned to fly to Panama in September, then set sail for New Orleans. After dinner at Antoine's they planned a rail trip to Indianapolis. With this letter, Nicholson enclosed a clipping from a Managua newspaper, complete with a photograph of himself that mentioned his expected nomination to be the next governor of Indiana. Without explaining the paper's misinformation, Nicholson said that Somoza was all for it and believed, having himself just visited West Lafayette, Indiana, that he "could hold the Purdue vote."[22]

Nicaragua was deemed a "hardship post" by the U.S. State Department for good reason. The accommodations for the diplomatic staff there were substandard, the climate was harsh (drought in the summer months and constant rains afterwards), and health concerns among the service personnel were unusually high. Both Nicholson and his wife suffered greatly in those conditions, but they held on as long as possible and continued to press forward the work of the legation. It was with particular pride that they watched from afar Somoza's visit to the United States in April and May 1939. Unfortunately, the press of business prevented them from joining the entourage.

Somoza began his North American visit by calling upon President Roosevelt, who welcomed the leader of a friendly Central American nation to Washington, approved the creation of a line of credit of some $2.5 million for "public improvements," and then accompanied the travelers (President and Mrs. Somoza, their daughter Lillian, and a few other officials) on a visit to Mount Vernon. The Nicaraguans had been received in Washington, D.C., with an impressive display of its military might—planes, tanks, and troops. (In part this was a dress rehearsal for a similar reception planned soon after for the British royal family—new King George VI, Queen Elizabeth, and their two daughters, Elizabeth and Margaret—who were then also touring North America.) Somoza's next stops were Philadelphia, where he had gone to school, and New York, after which he headed west, the ultimate goal being to attend the "world's fair" (officially the Golden Gate International Exposition) in San Francisco.

At Nicholson's suggestion and the mayor's official invitation, the Somoza group also stopped off briefly in Indianapolis and West Lafayette, where Somoza, interested in cattle raising, wanted to take an abbreviated version of the "agricultural course" at Purdue University. At first it seemed that time restraints would permit only one stop in Indiana, and West Lafayette was selected, in part also because Somoza's nephew, Luis Y. De Bayle, was then enrolled at Purdue studying chemical engineering.

A last-minute change, however, permitted the party to fit Indianapolis into its itinerary "for an hour." This revised schedule enabled Somoza "to make at least a courtesy call to the Hoosier capital as a compliment to Mr. Nicholson."[23]

When the train with special cars for the Somoza party pulled into Union Station about 8:00 a.m. on May 25, 1939, it was met by a reception committee that included the mayor, the governor, chamber of commerce officials, and Nicholson's three children, along with their spouses. Two university presidents, Edward Charles Elliott of Purdue University and Herman B Wells of Indiana University, and Nicholson's close friends, McCulloch, Stout, and William Fortune, were also among the reception committee. According to plans, the party proceeded from Union Station up Meridian Street to Monument Circle and then over to the statehouse before heading north again to the War Memorial. At the mayor's request, a number of blue and white Nicaraguan flags, along with American flags, were on display, hanging from downtown office buildings.[24]

In a surprise meeting at the War Memorial, four marines who had served in Nicaragua (to train Nicaraguan soldiers) and had been associated with Somoza as the head of the Nicaraguan National Guard were on hand to greet their former comrade-in-arms, who greatly enjoyed the brief reunion. Then, after a visit to the Shrine Room, which Somoza called the most "beautiful of its type he had ever seen," the party moved quickly out West Sixteenth Street to the Indianapolis Motor Speedway, where preparations were under way for the twenty-seventh running of the 500-Mile Race. There Somoza, reportedly once an automobile salesman in Philadelphia, jumped into the driver's seat of the pace car and sped around the track with a small group of astonished passengers, including three-time race winner Louie Meyer, Governor M. Clifford Townsend, the Nicaraguan minister of finance, and a race official. "And it was some ride, according to the Governor," wrote a reporter for the *Indianapolis News*. "He went ninety miles an hour, Townsend said," and the tires squealed as Somoza raced the car back into the pits.[25]

After this exciting finale to the Indianapolis visit, the party traveled more sedately by automobile up to West Lafayette, where the Purdue officials exhibited "typical Hoosier hospitality" amid impressive welcome ceremonies, a luncheon that included three Nicaraguan students then enrolled at Purdue, and an "intensive agricultural short course" for the president. This was to have included a milking contest between Somoza and Townsend, but while the president was "practicing," he "accidentally pointed the business end of the udder toward the Governor and ruined the scheduled contest when the Governor received a milk shower." According to the report, both "comedy and solemnity" had marked the visit to the university, and Somoza obviously delighted in both.[26]

Following the Somoza party's homecoming celebration in June, in which Nicholson participated, personal health concerns, compounded by Dorothy's complete breakdown early in 1940 that led her to seek treatment in California and included lengthy recuperation there in a sanitarium, persuaded Nicholson to consider resignation from foreign service. Perhaps his earliest thoughts about this had come in 1937, when he asked Chambers for the name of the best newspaper in Saint Augustine, Florida (the city to which the Nicholsons eventually retired in 1941), but for the moment he continued to do his job.[27]

An insight into the American legation at this point in Nicholson's career comes from Ernie Pyle when the self-styled "vagabond" reporter was on a tour of Central America. His syndicated column devoted five stories to Nicaragua, one on the city of Managua, which minced no words about the city's amenities, or lack thereof; and another on his dinner one evening with the American minister there. Concerning Managua, accessible to tourists only by air, he pointed out that the city's one "skyscraper" was a four-story building with Managua's only elevator—its two hotels were both two-story buildings—and its public transportation was by horse-drawn carriages. Oddly, too, the city water, supplied from a nearby volcanic crater, was "turned off about 10 at night and on again about 5 a.m." And Pyle called the telephone system "100 per cent mystic."[28]

Ernie Pyle served as a roving correspondent for the Scripps-Howard newspaper chain, producing a six-day-a-week column under the title "The Hoosier Vagabond."

Pyle obviously liked and admired Nicholson, "whose name is familiar to every inhabitant of the Hoosier state, and many millions more too, through his books." He said Nicholson had followed his "profession of letters for an average lifetime" and then, at age sixty-five, "he gave way to an old ambition to be a diplomat," representing "our country in various odd spots around the Western Hemisphere" for the past seven years. He described Nicholson as "fresh and neat" and "a large man, handsome of face" who had "a delightful sense of humor." Pyle also noted Dorothy's absence, euphemistically saying that she was then "vacationing" in California. Regarding the minister's residence, atop a knoll at the edge of Managua and near the airport, Pyle said that "a strong tropical wind whips through the house continuously. There are no glass windows, and the doors don't fit."[29] During dinner, Nicholson, "a willing and agile conversationalist," said he thought his guests, Americans all, were a cosmopolitan bunch, "so let's each call out what state he's from." Pyle was the last to speak, and when he said "Indiana" everyone laughed, "for that was Nicholson's point and he thought Indiana would win. But two of our fellow guests spoiled it by being from Virginia, so it came out a tie."[30]

After dinner, Nicholson showed his guests an old group photo of Riley, Ade, Tarkington, and Nicholson, "taken when they were young blades. It is one of the greatest pictures I ever saw." And he showed the group his collection of autographed photos in his bedroom—Tarkington and Riley again, John McCutcheon, Paul McNutt, and Roy Howard. Finally, shortly after 11 p.m. when all the guests departed, Nicholson "walked out to the cars with us, and he waved us goodby, standing there on the hilltop in the Nicaraguan darkness, with no friends except his servants, and I couldn't help feeling lonely for him." But, Pyle concluded, "if Nicholson truly is lonely down here, all he has to do is quit and go back to a state full of people who like him. And he can do it anytime he wants to, for he has paid the world already with a full, pleasant, and useful life, and he doesn't owe the world anything at all."[31]

Perhaps Nicholson took Pyle's parting comment to heart, for soon after going to California to visit Dorothy and bring her back with him to Managua, he submitted his resignation from the diplomatic service. All the ministers and ambassadors in the diplomatic service had been requested to do this at the end of the president's second term in office, in order to simplify reassignments for the next term. Nicholson clearly had mixed emotions—he wanted to be selected for continued service to boost his own morale, but he also knew it was time to go. So did Hull and Roosevelt, who thanked Nicholson for his service to his country and accepted the resignation. Nicholson must have been satisfied with this turn of events. He had told Dorothy in 1940, "I have had all I want of official life," and he later said he did not think he could survive another year in Managua. Consequently, in February 1941, a greatly relieved and much thinner Nicholson headed for home as the Nicholsons departed Latin America for the final time. Moreover, as he ruefully observed to McCulloch, "for the first time since I left school at the age of 15, I am out of a job."[32]

11

In Winter I Was Born

In winter I was born,
And as I came so let me pass away,
Out from the world on a December day
When the delaying morn.[1]

MEREDITH NICHOLSON, 1891

IMMEDIATELY UPON RETURNING FROM LATIN AMERICA, THEIR
home for the previous seven and one-half years, Meredith and Dorothy Nicholson moved into an apartment on
North Meridian Street in Indianapolis and tried to pick up
the pieces of their former lives. But theirs was an anoma-
lous situation; as Allegra Stewart put it, "doors that were
open" to Meredith and Eugenie Nicholson "were closed"
to Meredith and Dorothy Nicholson.[2] They had few
friends in common, the Nicholson family remained cool
to Dorothy, and overall the situation "back home again" in
Indiana was not meeting expectations.

Consequently, the itinerants looked to a retirement in
Florida, deciding (possibly for historical reasons) to live
in Saint Augustine, its founding date of 1565 making it
by far one of the oldest cities in North America. Nicholson was also pleased with his doctor there, a competent,
understanding man who treated the writer's usual old-age

ailments much as did his Indiana doctors, and who found it unnecessary to prescribe insulin for Nicholson's border-line diabetes. Meredith credited Dorothy with finding a nice rental house, "furnished in a civilized manner," at 70 Water Street, for their dwelling. Situated near the coast of Matanzas Bay, just north of the city's historic downtown and its late-seventeenth-century fort, the Castillo de San Marcos, this location kept the Nicholsons near the city center, including the old city gate, and able to take part in civic functions from time to time. When Hollywood actress Veronica Lake came to town on a tour to sell bonds, the Nicholsons heard the bands playing at the city gate, but they decided to avoid the crowds by listening to the hub-bub from their house and making a pledge by telephone rather than in person.

Other attractions of Saint Augustine were its many fine restaurants, including a Greek one where Nichol-son's honorary membership in two Greek letter societies (Phi Gamma Delta and Phi Beta Kappa) led the Greek owner to give him special service and favors. The Nichol-sons also happened to live near another celebrated writer, Marjorie Kinnan Rawlings, with whom they occasion-ally visited and dined out. They once also met the famed southern writer James Branch Cabell. But overall the Nicholsons were "disappointed" in Florida, both in terms of its climate (chillier in winter than anticipated) and its landscape. Moreover, "after hearing for years of the wonderful fertility of the soil we are shocked to find that the best oranges and all the produce we get here come from California and are so marked. Potatoes, etc., come from Texas and Georgia."[3]

Carleton B. McCulloch, in response, said that he "quite agreed" on the fertility of Florida's soil; moreover, he had a story to emphasize his point. "On my return from leaving Riley down at Miami, 'way back then,'" he wrote, "the train stopped at Saint Augustine while a bride and groom got on board, accompanied by rice, old shoes, etc. They had a stateroom and when the train reached Macon, I was called out of bed to help deliver her of a child. California has no such fertility as that."[4]

While still trying to make a go of it in Florida, Nicholson made his first public appearance to give a talk to the local Kiwanis group in December, shortly after the Japanese attack on the American fleet at Pearl Harbor. After first sharing his exchange of telegrams with President Anastasio Somoza in which Nicholson had congratulated the Nicaraguan leader for his prompt support of the United States in the war effort, Nicholson primarily spoke of his experiences in Latin America and what the life of an American diplomat involved. Somewhat to his surprise, he received very high marks for his talk, both from an army officer who called it "the finest speech he had ever heard" and in an unnamed Saint Augustine newspaper, which praised Nicholson's "eloquent and authentic discussion of our Good Neighbor Policy," adding that "he has an insight into Latin-American affairs that is unusual, because he made the approach to acquaintance there with the keen eye of a writer; one who is accustomed to read human nature; watch for details, and evaluate happenings."[5]

Nicholson also spoke to the Layman's League of the Episcopal Church a bit later on, as he tried to remain active in the community. In his usual self-deprecatory way, however, while reporting this activity to McCulloch, he pointed out that one of his auditors, the eighty-two-year-old local sheriff, had died the next day, "so I'm not saying much about my oratorical powers."[6]

The Nicholsons were also upset at being so close to wartime activities, occasionally hearing the sounds of naval battles as American naval vessels attacked coast-hugging German submarines and hearing about bodies being washed ashore. Nicholson added, "This absurd peninsular state is full of war activities—air, sea and land."[7] Consequently, after little more than a year in Florida, the Nicholsons returned to Indianapolis. They were worried about not being able to find suitable living quarters, given the tight wartime housing situation, but did find an apartment at 3310 North Meridian Street, and soon thereafter Nicholson began his biweekly column for the *Indianapolis Star*.

Although personal references from long ago often appeared in the columns, never did Nicholson mention his immediate day-to-day activities (or problems), nor did he draw upon his experiences in Latin America and his close contacts in the past with both the president and the secretary of state. The columns just began on April 19, 1943, and continued regularly, every Monday and Thursday, on the editorial page of the paper until suddenly, in early

Called "the most rabid of Hoosiers" by one Indiana literary historian, Nicholson devoted his life to cherishing a special bond between himself, his fellow Hoosiers, and his homeland.

November, they stopped without explanation other than a later editorial comment that accompanied an article about Nicholson by fellow columnist Jeannette Covert Nolan, explaining that Nicholson's column was missing because of an "illness" from which he was "recovering rapidly."[8] On December 23, Nicholson's column resumed, again without explanation by the author or his editors.

More curiously, it was during this period of Meredith's illness that Dorothy decided to end their marriage. Officially the divorce occurred on Christmas Eve, December 24, 1943, when Nicholson appeared in Judge Walter Pritchard's courtroom, announced the grounds for divorce—"it is embarrassing to say my wife says she no longer loves me"—and the proposed property settlement—an equal division of assets, which the judge promptly accepted and granted the divorce.[9] Nicholson's grandson has suggested that the court appearance was timed so that it would probably not be covered in the *Indianapolis News*. But if that was the intent, it did not succeed, for on Christmas Day there was a brief notice of Nicholson's courtroom appearance.

Thereafter, Nicholson lived alone at the Indianapolis Athletic Club while Dorothy remained in the apartment on North Meridian Street, at least temporarily. She summered in 1944 in Brutus, in northern Michigan, not far from Mackinac Island, but after that, nothing is known of her locations or activities.[10] It seems that she was an essential part of Nicholson's diplomatic activities, and enjoyed (perhaps at least once too much) her role as a representative of the United States in the three Latin American countries where they served. Upon their return to the America, however, Dorothy's role seemed to diminish; she felt ostracized in Indianapolis and eventually decided to leave. Unfortunately, too, still very little is known of Dorothy before 1933 or after 1944.[11]

Despite his uncertain health, Nicholson faithfully submitted the copy for his newspaper column, "Without Prejudice," on time. These columns maintained Nicholson's high standards in eloquence and accuracy and were quite well done. A combination of comments on current events, personal reflections on past events in Indiana history, and occasional profiles of interesting people, such as underappreciated writers like Maurice and Will Thompson and poet Benjamin House, "Without Prejudice" is a treasure trove of information about Indiana, Nicholson's philosophy, and his core values of piety, patriotism, democracy, and joie de vivre, all presented with his delightful sense of humor. Some of the columns were essays on a single topic, such as his idiosyncratic history of the Indianapolis Literary Club, and some were a collection of short paragraphs on random topics. Although he never did write a novel, as he once planned, on "The Rising Tide of Vulgarity in America," he did a column with that title on October 11, 1943.

The columns contain surprisingly little material that draw upon Nicholson's insights from having served abroad, although once, in an off-hand remark, he observed simply that "ambassadors and ministers are essentially report-ers." That comment helps explain Nicholson's success as a diplomat, for he could draw on his experiences as a reporter in order to write full and thoughtful accounts reporting and analyzing events in his assigned country. In other columns, after having reflected upon longevity and his own life, well past the biblical standard of three score and ten, he remarked that, if he could relive a por-tion of his life, he would choose "to repeat the 14 years I was employed on two Indianapolis newspapers. Though I served in other capacities, my adventures as a reporter were the most enjoyable."[12] Publication of Nicholson's columns continued into 1944, but ended forever on Sep-tember 7, 1944, evidently at the direction of the *Star*'s new publisher, Eugene Pulliam. Perhaps Pulliam wanted to get rid of such folksy contributions by Nicholson and Nolan, whose column alternated with Nicholson's on the editorial page and was also discontinued at this time, and offer his readers more hard news and fuller international coverage.[13]

A profile of Nicholson in the *Indianapolis Times*, writ-ten shortly after his return "home" from Latin American, gives an insight into the man in the fullness of his years.

The anonymous reporter began by saying that Nicholson, "famed author, world traveler and diplomat, rarely finds cornbread the way he wants it except in Indiana. The world's finest chefs haven't been able to break him of his idea that a good meal consists of country ham, home baked beans and cornbread." Then the profiler moved on to a physical description:

> Mr. Nicholson is now 74 years of age, a big (5 feet, 11 inches . . . 180 pounds) man with a magnificent carriage who carries his broad shoulders like a soldier. He has a striking face, square cut, with a jutting chin and determined expression.
>
> Dignified in manner, he sometimes gives the impression of austerity. On the contrary, his tastes are extremely simple and he is an immensely "human" person. He is one of Indiana's three or four best-known literary giants.

In a "warts and all" description, the reporter then honed in on one of Nicholson's vices, his smoking, which "always fascinated" visitors. "He smokes cigarettes chain style and talks with them in his mouth. His visitors can't take their eyes off the cigarette as the ash gets longer and longer without falling. Finally, it falls, usually on his vest."[14]

For one who publicly ridiculed exercise, often saying that countless friends of his had dropped dead on the golf course,

> [Nicholson's] idea of "proper exercise" is walking. He prefers the city's sidewalks to the country and the nearer the Circle the better he likes it. He always says he'd like to retire to a little farm to raise chickens and carrots, but his friends always laugh and say if ever there was a round peg in a square hole, "it would be Nick on a farm."
>
> Choosy about his clothing, he has all his suits tailor-made and yet for the last 20 years, he's hung on to a battered old gray felt hat, which he took to South America with him. He's had a lot of other hats in the meantime, but he always goes back to the old gray felt.
>
> He is one of those rare individuals who makes a real art of conversation. He loves to reminisce, but when he does, he has the ability to make his listeners actually live through the era. He would have made a magnificent history teacher. [15]

Lastly, in this lengthy profile, the reporter summarized Nicholson's life from his Crawfordsville birth through his numerous jobs, saying accurately that his time as a businessman in Colorado were the "unhappiest years of his

240

life." As a full-time writer beginning about forty years prior, however, Nicholson was eminently successful: "'Who's Who' lists 28 books of his, plus one play." The concluding paragraphs added a few personal details:

> He writes his stories and letters in longhand on foolscap paper in a beautiful script. He considers his essays his best work. Will Bobbs once referred to him as one of the very best of all literary technicians.
>
> He likes the radio, enjoys all kinds of music, particularly classical tunes. He is devoted to Elmer Davis. He likes movies. He reads a great deal at home, mostly history, biography and poetry and almost no fiction.
>
> And he thinks Indiana is the greatest place in the world. He likes to refer to i[t] as "The one-gallus, fried meat democracy."[16]

More intimate details concerning Nicholson's final years come from his daughter-in-law, Roberta West Nicholson, his most constant friend and ally at that time. Noting his increasing frailty and loneliness, she called upon him regularly at his lodgings at the Indianapolis Athletic Club, often bringing a favorite delicacy, oyster soup. She also mentioned, upon one such visit, that Nicholson was sweltering in his room because the electric fan was not working. Upon checking, she plugged it in and it ran fine. In response to her gentle rebuke about not knowing how to fix the problem, he said. "My dear, I'm a literary man, not a mechanical man."[17] Nicholson was also pictured in the newspaper late in life, perhaps his last photo being one with three relatives. This *Indianapolis News* photograph showed four generations of Nicholsons shortly after the revered author celebrated his eightieth birthday—Nicholson; his daughter, Elizabeth; his granddaughter, Jane Funk (Charles's daughter); and his great grandson, Jane's son, Neil Funk III.[18]

The end came slowly. On December 6, 1947, Nicholson slipped into a diabetic coma and was rushed to Methodist Hospital where, three days later, he revived enough to observe his eighty-first birthday and enjoy a small dish of ice cream. But twelve days later, on December 21, 1947, Nicholson died. It was sixteen years to the day following the death of his beloved first wife, and it also fulfilled his prophetic wish in the poem quoted above, to "pass away . . . on a December day." Funeral services, conducted by the Reverend William Burrows, Rector of St. Paul's Episcopal Church, at the Flanner and Buchanan Mortuary preceded interment at Crown Hill Cemetery. There were no active pallbearers, but the twenty-seven honorary pallbearers comprised a list of distinguished men from Indiana and elsewhere, including Carleton B. McCulloch, David L. Chambers, J. K. Lilly, Paul V. McNutt, Roy Howard, and Wabash College president Frank H. Sparks.

The obituaries that spread across local and national newspapers would have made Nicholson, as an unreformed newspaperman himself, proud of his colleagues for their fullness and their accuracy in these stories. But the *New York Times* said it best, calling Nicholson the "last leaf on a famous literary tree that grew in Indiana. It was a sturdy tree, pleasant and shady, watered in the American tradition with its roots deep in the soil of the state. In its day, it was one of the outstanding features of our literary landscape."[19]

It seems appropriate, given Nicholson's penchant for ending writings of his own with some lines of poetry or apt quotations, to do the same here. One might use a favorite Nicholson quotation from Matthew Arnold, who said that one's goal should be "to see life steadily and see it whole," or from Walt Whitman, "Produce great men, the rest follows." The words of Charles Lamb, however, which provided the title of Nicholson's last book, seem best:

I have had playmates, I have had companions,
In my days of childhood, in my joyful school-days—
All, all are gone, the old familiar faces.

I have been laughing, I have been carousing,
Drinking late, sitting late, with my bosom cronies—
All, all are gone, the old familiar faces.

I loved a Love once, fairest among women;
Closed are her doors on me, I must not see her—
All, all are gone, the old familiar faces.
I have a friend, a kinder friend has no man:
Like an ingrate, I left my friend abruptly;
Left him, to muse on the old familiar faces.

Ghost-like I paced round the haunts of my childhood,
Earth seem'd a desert I was bound to traverse,
Seeking to find the old familiar faces.

Friend of my bosom, thou more than a brother,
Why wert not thou born in my father's dwelling?
So might we talk of the old familiar faces—

How some they have died, and some they have left me,
And some are taken from me; all are departed—
All, all are gone, the old familiar faces.[20]

Introduction

1. Meredith Nicholson, "Stand Up for Indiana," *Indianapolis News*, July 3, 1917.

2. Ibid.; Dorothy Ritter Russo and Thelma Lois Sullivan, comps. *Bibliographical Studies of Seven Authors of Crawfordsville, Indiana: Lew and Susan Wallace, Maurice and Will Thompson, Mary Hannah and Caroline Virginia Krout, and Meredith Nicholson* (Indianapolis: Indiana Historical Society, 1952), 69–172 (the quotation is at 71).

3. Kin Hubbard, ed., *A Book of Indiana: The Story of What Has Been Described as the Most Typically American State in the American Democracy Told in Terms of Biography* (Indianapolis: Indiana Biographical Association, 1929), 5.

4. Arthur W. Shumaker, *A History of Indiana Literature, with Emphasis on the Authors of Imaginative Works Who Commenced Writing Prior to World War II* (Indianapolis: Indiana Historical Society, 1962), 325; Meredith Nicholson, "Indianapolis: A City of Homes," *Atlantic Monthly* 93 (June 1904): 836–45, reprinted in part in Ralph D. Gray, ed., *The Hoosier State: Readings in Indiana History*, 2 vols. (Grand Rapids, MI: Wm. B. Erdmann's Company, 1980), 2:27–37.

Chapter 1

1. Meredith Nicholson, "One's Grandfather," *Old Familiar Faces* (Indianapolis: Bobbs-Merrill Company, 1929), 15.

2. See also the unpublished manuscript by Allegra Stewart, "Meredith Nicholson Revisited" (1988), Allegra Stewart Papers,

Special Collections, Rare Books, and University Archives, Irwin Library, Butler University, Indianapolis, especially chapter two; John W. Miller, *Indiana Newspaper Bibliography: Historical Accounts of All Indiana Newspapers Published from 1804 to 1980 and Locational Information for All Available Copies, Both Original and Microfilm* (Indianapolis: Indiana Historical Society, 1982), 488–89; and Kate Milner Rabb, "Hoosier Listening Post," *Indianapolis Star*, October 21 and 22, 1932.

3. The primary sources of information about Edward Willis Nicholson's military service during the Civil War are in his pension records file in the National Archives and Records Administration, Washington, D.C. Some of these records, evidently mistakenly, refer to Nicholson as a deserter when, for health reasons, he missed certain roll calls, but his service afterwards as an artillery officer suggests that he was indeed a loyal Union army soldier who was mustered out of service in July 1865. The best account of Indiana's role in the Civil War is by Emma Lou Thornbrough, *Indiana in the Civil War Era, 1850–1880* (Indianapolis: Indiana Historical Bureau and Indiana Historical Society, 1965), chapters 3, 4, and 5 (the quotation is at 148). See in particular Meredith Nicholson's poems on the war, such as "On the Battlefield at Antietam" (1910), and "Shiloh" and "The Heart of the Bugle" in *Poems* (Indianapolis: Bobbs-Merrill Company, 1906). See also his front-page poem welcoming the Grand Army of the Republic to its convention in Indianapolis in the *Indianapolis News*, September 4, 1893.

4. The heavy incidence of post-traumatic stress disorders (PTSD), including alcoholism, depression, insanity, and suicide, among Civil War and Vietnam War veterans has been vividly portrayed in Eric T. Dean, Jr., *Shook Over Hell: Post-Traumatic Stress, Vietnam, and the Civil War* (Cambridge, MA: Harvard University Press, 1997). Dean studied 291 cases of Indiana Civil War veterans (the Indiana Sample) who had been committed to Central State Hospital in Indianapolis, most of whom suffered from "what we would today think of as PTSD, of both the acute and delayed type" (70). Their experiences often were not unlike those of Captain Nicholson.

5. Nicholson, *Old Familiar Faces*, 89; Meredith Nicholson to May Shipp, September 18, 1894, Roberta West Nicholson Collection, Manuscript Division, Indiana State Library, Indianapolis.

Chapter 2

1. Meredith Nicholson, "Without Benefit of College," *Old Familiar Faces* (Indianapolis: Bobbs-Merrill Company, 1929), 85.

2. Ibid., chapter 1; Dorothy Ritter Russo and Thelma Lois Sullivan, *Bibliographical Studies of Seven Authors of Crawfordsville, Indiana: Lew and Susan Wallace, Maurice and Will Thompson, Mary Hannah and Caroline Virginia Krout, and Meredith Nicholson* (Indianapolis: Indiana Historical Society, 1952), passim.

3. Nicholson, *Old Familiar Faces*, 90–91; William S. McFeely, *Grant: A Biography* (New York: W. W. Norton, 1981), 450–477; Meredith Nicholson to Luther L. Dickenson, February 2, 1943, quoted in Cathy Gibson, "The Vagaries of Memories," *Reading in Indianapolis: Newsletter of the Indianapolis-Marion County Public Library* (October 15–31, 1995), 1–2. This letter served the purpose of the author's point about memory, for Nicholson had forgotten the year, not of course the day and month, of his meeting with Grant, and Dickerson had supplied it.

4. In addition to the major essay "Without Benefit of College" in *Old Familiar Faces*, see Nicholson, "A Hoosier Boyhood," *Youth's Companion*, December 9, 1915, reprinted in Charity Dye, *Some Torch Bearers in Indiana* (Indianapolis: The Hollenbeck Press, 1917), 276–82; Nicholson, "An Autobiographical Chapter," *Indianapolis Star*, January 30, 1916; Meredith Nicholson, "A Brief Story of His Life Told by Himself," *Indianapolis Sunday Star*, October 20, 1918 (reprinted from a recent *Collier's Magazine* at the head of a new five-part serial by Nicholson); and Nicholson's responses on an undated, post–World War I author's questionnaire in the Bobbs-Merrill Papers, Lilly Library, Indiana University.

5. Nicholson, *Old Familiar Faces*, 86–88. Presumably the move to Colorado came when Emily Meredith Nicholson joined her son and his family in Denver, where they lived from 1898 to 1901.

6. Lawrence J. Downey, *A Live Thing in the Whole Town: The History of the Indianapolis-Marion County Public Library, 1873–1990* (Indianapolis: Indianapolis Marion County Public Library Foundation, 1991), 20 (quotation) and passim.

7. Charles Evans, "Looking Backward: An Address Before the Indianapolis Literary Club on Their Fiftieth Anniversary, January 10,

1927, by Charles Evans," in Raymond E. Gnat, comp., and Lawrence S. Connor, ed., *The Indianapolis Literary Club: Summarized Record, 1976–2003; To Which is Appended Historical Reminiscences and Vignettes* (Indianapolis: Indianapolis Literary Club Foundation, 2004), 112–17, quotation at 116.

8. The fullest account of this episode is in Dye, *Some Torch Bearers in Indiana*, 276–77.

9. Nicholson, *Old Familiar Faces*, 97. The drugstore was the "Cole Bros. drug emporium at Ill[inois] & Wash[ington]—n.e. cor[ner]—where I worked Sat[urday] and Sunday." Meredith Nicholson to Carleton B. McCulloch, January 12, 1935, Carleton B. McCulloch Papers, William Henry Smith Memorial Library, Indiana Historical Society, Indianapolis. Today that is the site of a new hotel, the Conrad, adjacent to the Artsgarden, a prime location in the heart of Indianapolis.

10. Nicholson, *Old Familiar Faces*, 108. For Nicholson's fond memories of Lew Wallace, see "Lew Wallace as Meredith Nicholson Knew Him," *Indianapolis Sunday Star*, January 9, 1910, and the earlier appreciation in Meredith Nicholson, *The Hoosiers* (New York: Macmillan, 1915), 180–199.

11. Nicholson, *Old Familiar Faces*, 97–99.

12. Ibid., 99–100.

13. Ibid., 93–94. Reed (1836–99) left Indianapolis in 1884 to fill the pulpit in an affluent church in Denver, Colorado. His "radical" Christian Socialism views, however, led to his resignation in 1894, after which, at the urgings of his supporters, he started a new church, the independent Broadway Temple, where he served until his death. Reed was also a very close friend of James Whitcomb Riley, and the two had once traveled abroad together in the 1890s. For a full account of Reed's life, see James A. Denton, *Rocky Mountain Radical: Myron W. Reed, Christian Socialist* (Albuquerque: University of New Mexico Press, 1997).

14. Nicholson, *Old Familiar Faces*, 109–11.

15. Ibid., 111–12. Bone went on to successful careers in both journalism and politics. For a number of years he was an editor for the *Washington Post* and then owned and edited his own paper in the nation's capital. In 1916 he was a delegate to the Republican National Convention in Chicago and helped nominate a fellow Hoosier, Charles W.

Fairbanks, for the vice presidency. Subsequently Bone moved to Seattle, Washington, became involved in Alaskan territorial politics, and served a term as governor of the Alaska Territory, 1921–25. *Who Was Who in America*, 1: 115; Allegra Stewart, "Meredith Nicholson Revisited" (1988), Allegra Stewart Papers, Special Collections, Rare Books, and University Archives, Irwin Library, Butler University, Indianapolis, chapter 2. There has been some confusion about the timing of Nicholson's earliest employments. According to John W. Miller, *Indiana Newspaper Bibliography: Historical Accounts of All Indiana Newspapers Published from 1804 to 1980 and Locational Information for All Available Copies, both Original and Microfilm* (Indianapolis: Indiana Historical Society, 1982), 276, Matthews and Bone came to the *Indianapolis Sentinel* in "early July, 1886." Since Nicholson joined the paper at that time, we can pinpoint the time he became a newsman.

Chapter 3

1. Untitled poem in Meredith Nicholson's hand, February 8, 1893, Roberta West Nicholson Collection, Manuscript Division, Indiana State Library, Indianapolis.

2. Edward A. Leary, *Indianapolis: The Story of a City* (Indianapolis: Bobbs-Merrill Company, 1970), 135–47; see also George W. Geib, *Indianapolis: Hoosiers' Circle City* (Tulsa, OK: Continental Heritage Press, 1981).

3. Leary, *Indianapolis*, 137.

4. The Bone comment is in the Allegra Stewart Papers, Special Collections, Rare Books, and University Archives, Irwin Library, Butler University, Indianapolis.

5. Yancy Deering, "Simeon Coy," in David J. Bodenhamer and Robert G. Barrows, eds., *Encyclopedia of Indianapolis*, (Bloomington and Indianapolis: Indiana University Press, 1994), 480–81.

6. Meredith Nicholson, "Hoosier Reminisces in Far-Away Caracas," *Indianapolis News*, February 5, 1936.

7. *Indianapolis News*, June 13, 1890.

8. Ibid., September 4, 1893.

9. Dorothy Ritter Russo and Thelma Lois Sullivan, eds., *Biographical Studies of Seven Authors of Crawfordsville, Indiana: Lew and Susan Wallace, Maurice and Will Thompson, Mary Hannah and*

Caroline Virginia Kraut, and Meredith Nicholson (Indianapolis: Indiana Historical Society, 1952), 154–72.

10. For information about the club, see Raymond E. Gnat, comp., and Lawrence S. Connor, ed., *The Indianapolis Literary Club: Summarized Record, 1976–2003; To Which is Appended Historical Reminiscences and Vignettes* (Indianapolis: Indianapolis Literary Club Foundation, 2004); see also Nicholson's reflections on the club's history in his newspaper column, "Without Prejudice," *Indianapolis Star*, March 2, 1944. This essay, "An Ancient and Honorable Society," was also reprinted in the club history cited above, 126–28.

11. Although *Short Flights* carries an 1891 date, it actually appeared late in 1890, and the *Indianapolis News* reviewed the one-hundred-page book on December 24, 1890. The quotation is in Meredith Nicholson to Josephine Piercy, March 2, 1925, Josephine Piercy Papers, Manuscripts Department, Lilly Library, Indiana University, Bloomington.

12. Meredith Nicholson, ed., *Poems of Benjamin D. House* (Indianapolis: Carlon and Hollenbeck, 1892). A different tribute by Nicholson, basically an obituary, appeared in the Western Association of Writers', *A Souvenir of the Fourth Annual Convention at Warsaw, Indiana* (Richmond, IN: M. Cullaton and Company, 1890).

13. Meredith Nicholson, *Old Familiar Faces* (Indianapolis: Bobbs-Merrill Company, 1929), 114.

14. Ibid., 112–13. When May Shipp died in 1960, her obituary identified her in its headline as a "friend of Riley." A longtime reader for the Bobbs-Merrill Company, Shipp also helped found the Indianapolis Dramatic Club and the Progressive Club. For more information, see her obituary in the *Indianapolis News*, May 5, 1960.

15. Meredith Nicholson to Mrs. Judah, Judah-Brandon Family Papers, 1820–1950, William Henry Smith Memorial Library, Indiana Historical Society, Indianapolis.

16. Nicholson to "My dear Mrs. Judah," October 27, 1892, ibid.

17. See Meredith Nicholson to Robert Underwood Johnson, February 26, 1898, Meredith Nicholson Collection, Clifton Walker Barrett Library, Special Collections, University of Virginia Library, Charlottesville.

18. Meredith Nicholson to Louis Vernon Ledoux, January 13 [1931], George E. Woodberry Papers, Rare Book and Manuscript Library, Columbia University. Unfortunately, very little of the correspondence between the two poets has survived, but there are twelve letters from Woodberry to Nicholson in Walter de la Mare, ed., *Selected Letters of George Edward Woodberry* (Boston: Houghton Mifflin Company, 1933).

19. Meredith Nicholson to "My dearest Harry," November 30, 1894, Judah-Brandon Family Papers. Evidently Harry was the familiar name of Henry Judah Brandon, whose "picaresque career" was summarized by Charles Latham in his "historical sketch" at the front of the guide to the Judah-Brandon Family Collection at the IHS library. Brandon, the son of John and Mary Judah, agreed (for a handsome price) to change his name to Brandon, his grandmother's maiden name, and was attending Yale and then law school in Chicago in the mid-1890s.

20. Kenyon Nicholson moved to New York in his youth and became a successful playwright with many Broadway hits to his credit, beginning with *The Barker*, starring Claudette Colbert. Much younger than Meredith, he teasingly called him "Uncle Meredith," although their only ties were a common hometown and connections to Wabash College, from which Kenyon graduated in 1917. Stanley J. Kunitz and Howard Haycraft, eds., *Twentieth Century Authors: A Biographical Dictionary of Modern Literature* (New York: The H. W. Wilson Company, 1942), 1023–24. As a young man Nicholson appeared in "blackface," singing and dancing before three thousand spectators at the Murat Theater while dressed in a loud checkered jacket, dark pants, and spats.

21. Meredith Nicholson to "My dear Mrs. Judah," March 1, 1893, Judah-Brandon Family Papers.

22. Ibid.

23. Ibid.

24. Herman Kountze's brothers followed similar career paths, leaving Ohio for the West while seeking likely places to establish banks. Meredith Nicholson III Files, Casa Grande, Arizona; Allegra Stewart, "Meredith Nicholson Revisited" (1988), chapter 5, Allegra Stewart Papers.

25. Meredith Nicholson to "My Dear Friends," September 30, 1895, Judah-Brandon Family Papers.

26. Ibid., April 29, 1896.

27. According to the *Omaha World-Herald*, June 16, 1896, Nicholson family members who attended the wedding were the groom's mother and an uncle from Chicago, William Morton Meredith. Oddly, however, this story identified Nicholson as "one of the foremost men" of Indianapolis in charge of the "foreign policy" of the *Indianapolis News*.

28. Meredith Nicholson to "My Dear Friends," March 19, 1896, Judah-Branson Family Papers; the people Nicholson jokingly referred to were, in addition to Russian tsar Nicholas II, the prime minister of Italy, Francisco Crispi, and the king of Ethiopia, Menelik II, who claimed to be descended from Solomon and the Queen of Sheba.

Chapter 4

1. *Indianapolis News*, September 18, 1925.

2. George C. Calvert to Margaret Ashley Todd, July 22, 1898, Holland Papers, Lilly Library, Indiana University, Bloomington.

3. Evidence of his early job-hunting in eastern cities is in Meredith Nicholson to "My dear Stoddard," April 24, 1898, Meredith Nicholson Collection, Manuscript Division, Indiana State Library, Indianapolis.

4. Meredith Nicholson, "An Ancient and Honorable Society [The Indianapolis Literary Club]," *Indianapolis Star*, March 2, 1944, reprinted in Raymond E. Gnat, comp., and Lawrence S. Connor, eds., *The Indianapolis Literary Club: Summarized Record, 1976–2003; To Which is Appended Historical Reminiscences and Vignettes* (Indianapolis: Indianapolis Literary Club Foundation, 2004), 126–28. The information on the family is from the private papers of Meredith Nicholson III, Casa Grande, Arizona.

5. Walter de la Mare, ed., *Selected Letters of George Edward Woodberry* (Boston: Houghton Mifflin Company, 1933), 23; the letter to Nicholson was dated December 31, 1900. For a brief appreciation of Nicholson's book, see Ralph D. Gray, "Indiana Bookshelf: The Centennial of *The Hoosiers*," *Traces of Indiana and Midwestern History* 12

(Fall 2000): 42–44. The only state history in print at the time of Nicholson's research was William Henry Smith, *The History of the State of Indiana from the Earliest Explorations to the Present Time* (Indianapolis: B. L. Blair, 1897), but there is no evidence of its use by Nicholson. He did profit from the availability of the early publications of the newly revived Indiana Historical Society, which included Jacob Piatt Dunn's study of the word "Hoosiers"; Dunn's *Indiana: A Redemption from Slavery* (Boston: Houghton Mifflin, 1888); Richard G. Boone, *A History of Education in Indiana* (New York: D. Appleton, 1892); and some early county and town histories.

    6. Meredith Nicholson, *The Hoosiers* (New York: Macmillan, 1900), vii–viii, 88–94, quotations at 89 and 92.

    7. Ibid., 18.

    8. Ibid., vii, 27–28.

    9. Ibid., 46–47. See also Nicholson's letter to May Louise Shipp regarding his expectation of having to defend his "so-called Hoosier dialect" remark, January 7, 1901, Roberta West Nicholson Collection, Manuscript Division, Indiana State Library, Indianapolis.

    10. Interestingly, one of the early ministers about whom Nicholson wrote was the Reverend George Bush (1796–1859), who also was a character, Dr. Shrub, in the important but satiric book by Baynard Rush Hall, *The New Purchase; or, Seven and a Half Years in the Far West* (New York: D. Appleton, 1843). Nicholson discussed this book, subsequently reprinted by Princeton University Press in one volume in 1916, at length, identifying Bush and many other people and places referred to by Hall under pseudonyms. Hall also used a penname for himself, Robert Carlton, supposedly the author of *The New Purchase*. Hall had been one of the first professors to teach at Indiana College before it became Indiana University in 1838.

    11. Quoted in Gray, "Centennial of *The Hoosiers*," 44. Sampson's review had appeared in March 1901.

    12. Meredith Nicholson to May Louise Shipp, January 7, 1901, Roberta West Nicholson Collection.

    13. *Indianapolis Journal*, December 2, 1900.

    14. Ibid., December 16, 1900.

    15. Ibid.

    16. *Indianapolis News*, November 24, 1900.

17. Ibid., December 5, 1900.

18. Ibid.

19. Ibid.

20. See Meredith Nicholson to May Louise Shipp, March 15, 1901, Roberta West Nicholson Collection, for a brief mention of the recent troubles—"it seems things can never go on as before"; see also Meredith Nicholson to "My Dearest Genie," May 5, 1901, Indiana History Papers, Lilly Library, Indiana University, for his complaints about life in Denver.

21. Meredith Nicholson to Eugenie Nicholson, May 16, 1901, Indiana History Papers.

22. Meredith Nicholson to Eugenie Nicholson, May 20 and May 31, 1901, ibid. The Nicholsons had little Eugenie reinterred in Crown Hill Cemetery in 1902, the year after Nicholson wrote a twelve-stanza poem, "She Gathers Roses," in her memory. Writing that "the autumn gave her," but "her eyes knew never spring's enchantment sweet," Nicholson ended the poem with the thought that in Heaven's "love-lighted garden-lands / She wanders with untroubled heart, / and gathers roses in her hands." See Meredith Nicholson, *Poems* (Indianapolis: Bobbs-Merrill Company, 1906), 92–94.

23. Meredith Nicholson to Eugenie Nicholson, June 10, 1901, Indiana History Papers.

24. Ibid., n.d. [September 1901?].

Chapter 5

1. Meredith Nicholson, *The Main Chance* (Indianapolis: Bobbs-Merrill Company, 1903), 17. In many ways, this description of a character in the novel is close to a self-portrait of the author.

2. Allegra Stewart, "Meredith Nicholson Revisited" (1988), chapter 2, Allegra Stewart Papers, Special Collections, Rare Books, and University Archives, Irwin Library, Butler University, Indianapolis.

3. Meredith Nicholson, "Edward Eggleston," *Atlantic Monthly* 90 (December 1902): 804–9. The poem is in the same volume at 440.

4. "Authors Faced Great Audience," *Indianapolis News*, May 31, 1902.

5. "Indiana's Success in Literature Discussed in a Boston Newspaper," *Indianapolis News*, May 31, 1902. In 1907 President Theodore

Roosevelt, also a famed Spanish-American War veteran, attended the unveiling of a statue memorializing General Lawton in downtown Indianapolis that has since been moved to Garfield Park.

6. "Authors Faced Great Audience."

7. The standard biography of Harrison is the three-volume study by Harry J. Sievers, *Benjamin Harrison* (Chicago: Henry H. Regnery, [1959–68]). For a brief summary of the lawyer-soldier-politician's career, see Donald L. Kinzer, "Benjamin Harrison and the Politics of Availability," in Ralph D. Gray, ed., *Gentlemen from Indiana: National Party Candidates, 1836–1940* (Indianapolis: Indiana Historical Bureau, 1977), 141–69.

8. "Authors Faced Great Audience." The full text of Riley's poem can be found in *The Complete Poetical Works of James Whitcomb Riley* (Garden City, NJ: Garden City Publishing Company, 1941), 409–10.

9. "Authors Faced Great Audience." This was actually Nicholson's second such appearance in a benefit reading by a group of authors. His first such experience had come in 1893, shortly after his initial book of poetry appeared. Other readers at this Indianapolis press club benefit were Kentuckian Douglass Sherley, famous as one of Riley's touring partners, Wallace, and Riley. See "The Press Club Benefit," *Indianapolis Journal*, June 22, 1893.

10. The information about the use of a pseudonym when submitting his first novel is contained in a news story announcing the book's appearance. See "A New Novel by Meredith Nicholson, 'The Main Chance,' Is Just Issued by Publishers," *Indianapolis News*, May 14, 1903.

11. Nicholson, *Main Chance*, 99, 109.

12. Ibid., 1.

13. "Meredith Nicholson's New Novel, "The Main Chance," *Indianapolis News*, May 16, 1903.

14. "The Main Chance," *Indianapolis Journal*, May 17, 1903.

15. Nicholson, *Main Chance*, 80.

16. [Meredith Nicholson], "Tale of a Postage Stamp," *Chicago Tribune*, February 20, 1886.

17. *Indianapolis Journal*, November 11, 1903.

18. Nicholson, *Zelda Dameron* (Indianapolis: Bobbs-Merrill Company, 1904), passim.

19. *Indianapolis Star*, November 15, 1903.

Chapter 6

1. Meredith Nicholson, *The House of a Thousand Candles* (Indianapolis: Bobbs-Merrill Company, 1905), 42–43.

2. Nicholson and George Barr McCutcheon discussed their methods of work in "Secrets of Greatness of Two Indiana Authors," *Indianapolis Star*, December 6, 1908. Later, in the foreword to a reprinting of a favorite story, Nicholson gave the fullest explanation of his writing techniques (see Ray Long, ed., *My Story That I Like Best* (New York: International Magazine Company, 1925), 173–76).

3. Ibid.; Meredith Nicholson, author's questionnaire, Bobbs-Merrill MSS., Lilly Library, Indiana University, Bloomington.

4. Englishman Anthony Hope, actually Anthony Hope Hawkins, was a near contemporary of Meredith Nicholson and both became prolific authors after abandoning promising business careers. Hope's *The Prisoner of Zenda*, considered by many "the finest adventure story ever written," was enormously successful and the inspiration for dozens of imitations. The original farce was "a captivating fairy tale about how a gentleman, masquerading as the King of Ruritania, a fictional eastern European kingdom, won the heart of a beautiful princess" while also defeating "the nefarious schemes of an evil duke." Frequently dramatized and several times made into a motion picture, most famously the production in 1937 starring Ronald Colman, Madeleine Carroll, Raymond Massey, and Douglas Fairbanks. Jr., *The Prisoner of Zenda* continued its popularity for generations. (Gary Hoppenstand, introduction to *The Prisoner of Zenda, Being the History of Three Months in the Life of an English Gentleman*, by Anthony Hope (New York: Penguin, 1999), vii–viii, xx.)

5. Nicholson, *The House of a Thousand Candles*, 8, 34, 378–79.

6. See Meredith Nicholson to the Culver High School Annual, January 24, 1930, in *The Maxinkuckee: Culver High School Annual* (1930), 6. The author is grateful to Judy McCollough, Historical Archives Manager at the Marshall County Historical Society in Plymouth, Indiana, for supplying me with a photocopy of this letter, and to Craighton Hippenhammer, current owner of The House of a Thousand Candles in Culver, for the referral to her.

7. *New York Herald*, September 23, 1906, as quoted in Dorothy Ritter Russo and Thelma Lois Sullivan, *Bibliographical Studies of Seven*

Authors of Crawfordsville, Indiana: Lew and Susan Wallace, Maurice and Will Thompson, Mary Hannah and Caroline Virginia Krout, and Meredith Nicholson (Indianapolis: Indiana Historical Society, 1952), 89.

8.   Nicholson, *House of a Thousand Candles*, 3.

9.   Ibid., 18, 20.

10. *Boston Transcript*, November 15, 1911.

11.   Another descendant of William M. Meredith and a niece of the assassinated William L. Meredith, Margaret Arrington of Edgewater, Maryland, provided copies of her extensive file of newspaper clippings that detail the long, troubled relationship between her uncle and his assassin, John Considine. She also referred me to a book that devotes most of a long chapter to this relationship: Murray Morgan, *Skid Road: An Informal Portrait of Seattle*, rev. ed. (New York: Ballantine Books, 1960). The author is appreciative of her assistance. Of course, all the Seattle newspapers covered the murder, but see especially "Ex-Chief of Police W. L. Meredith Shot and Killed by John W. Considine," *Seattle Post-Intelligencer*, June 26, 1901, and various follow-up articles.

12.   Meredith Nicholson to Roger L. Scaife, May 27, 1915, Houghton Mifflin Company Papers, Houghton Library, Harvard University, Cambridge, Massachusetts.

13.   *New York Times*, December 16, 1905.

14.   Hippenhammer Collection, Culver, Indiana. Craighton Hippenhammer is the current owner of the house on Lake Maxinkuckee that bears the name House of a Thousand Candles, and he is deeply interested in its history and connection to Nicholson. Hippenhamer supplied the author the information about the identity of the little girl in the red tam o'shanter who lived near Nicholson. He learned of this directly from Charles Latham Jr., who in fact had told the author this story many years ago, without the corroborating details he graciously supplied to Hippenhammer, so the author discounted the story. Nicholson mentioned the fortuitous and timely appearance of "that young lady, who, on the day I began the story, as I waited for the ink to thaw in my workshop, passed under my window, by one of those kindly orderings of Providence" in his essay, "Confessions of a Best-Seller," *Atlantic Monthly* (November 1909), reprinted in Meredith Nicholson, *The Provincial American and Other Papers* (Boston: Houghton Mifflin Company, 1912), 205–37, quotation at 213.

15. *In Memoriam Major General Lew Wallace* (Indianapolis: Loyal Legion, 1905). A full citation, listing all the authors, is in Russo and Sullivan, comps., *Biographical Studies of Seven Authors of Crawfordsville, Indiana*, 143. Nicholson's essay differs from his other writings on Wallace in *The Hoosiers* (1900), the *Atlantic Monthly* (March 1911), and *The Reader Magazine* (April 1905).

16. This essay, titled "Indianapolis; A City of Homes," appeared in the December 1905 issue of the magazine and, despite its gentle tone, was a determined defense of the author's adopted home city.

17. "A Virginia Impression: Washington and Lee." *The Phi Gamma Delta* (November 1905), 72–77.

18. Quoted in the *Indianapolis Star*, May 2, 1906.

19. The house was built by Harriet and Walter Newberry, a hops peddler from Detroit and Chicago and later a congressman from Illinois. Subsequent owners included the Bimms of Dayton, Ohio, and perhaps the Nicholsons. Later, Julius Stroh of the Stroh Brewing Company of Detroit bought the house. Stroh doubled the house's size before passing it on to Armin Rickel, owner of the Rickel Malt Company of Detroit. Rickel descendents still own the house. Susan Stites and Lea Ann Sterling, *Historic Cottages of Mackinac Island* (Mayfield, MI: Arbutus Press, 2001), 46. See also Phil Porter, *View from the Veranda: The History and Architecture of the Summer Cottages on Mackinac Island* (Lansing, MI: Mackinac State Historic Parks, 1981), and Phil Porter to Beth V. Gray, August 30, 2004, in the author's files. Porter is the director of the Mackinac State Historic Parks.

20. Meredith Nicholson to James Whitcomb Riley, August 20 and September 19, 1906, Riley Papers, Lilly Library, Indiana University. Carleton B. McCulloch, who accompanied Nicholson abroad on a second trip, corroborated Nicholson's implied statement of being unable to master pounds, shillings, and pence. McCulloch said Nicholson tended to give away the smaller, more valuable coins, thereby constantly overpaying. Nicholson's companions took over all financial dealings so that Nicholson could travel comfortably and stay solvent. See McCulloch, "A Tribute of an Old Friend," *Indianapolis Star*, September 5, 1933.

21. Meredith Nicholson, *Poems* (Indianapolis: Bobbs-Merrill Company, 1906).

22. "Indiana Dedicates Shaft at Antietam," *Indianapolis News*, September 17, 1910.

23. This untitled work appeared in the *Indianapolis News*, March 5, 1913, along with extensive coverage of the Wilson-Marshall inaugural ceremonies for Woodrow Wilson and Thomas Marshall.

24. Meredith Nicholson to James Whitcomb Riley, May 25, 1906, Riley Papers. The copy of Nicholson's *Poems* in the Huntington Library, Art Collection, and Botanical Garden, San Marino, California, bears an inscription "for Charles Ramm Esq." that reads: "The dedication of this volume to Riley was in appreciation of his friendship and in recognition of his encouragement and inspiration. As will appear from a sketch I printed in the Atlantic Monthly shortly after his death, I knew him very intimately. He was the dearest of men, and I profited greatly by his counsel. It may very truly be said that to know him was to love him. Meredith Nicholson Indianapolis July 5, 1919."

25. "Read the Bible Says Meredith Nicholson," *Indianapolis News*, January 20, 1909; see also Russo and Sullivan, *Seven Authors of Crawfordsville, Indiana*, 144, 154–72, for listings of Nicholson items in the press and elsewhere, including *Who's Who in America*, at this time.

26. *The Arena* 39 (January 1908): 145 and *The Nation* 86 (January 16, 1908): 162, as quoted in the *Book Review Digest* (1908): 266.

27. *New York Times*, October 30, 1908, *The American Library Association Booklet* 4 (October 1908): 241; and *The Arena* 40 (November 1908): 481, as quoted in the *Book Review Digest* (1908): 266. The reviews for two Nicholson books were summarized on the same page that year.

28. Meredith Nicholson to James Whitcomb Riley, August 20, 1906, Riley Papers. The ambition, "some day to write a pretty good book," is repeated in Meredith Nicholson to Julius Chambers, February 2, 1907, Robert Bridges Papers, Lilly Library.

Chapter 7

1. Meredith Nicholson, "Confessions of a Best-Seller," *Atlantic Monthly* (November 1909), reprinted in Meredith Nicholson, *The Provincial American and Other Papers* (Boston and New York: Houghton Mifflin Company, 1912), 236–37.

2. The results of John H. Moriarity's study, first reported in the *Indiana Quarterly for Bookmen* 3 (January 1947), and later revised by the author, have been summarized in R. E. Banta, *Indiana Authors and Their Books, 1816–1916: Biographical Sketches of Authors Who Published During the First Century of Indiana Statehood, With Lists of Their Books* (Crawfordsville, IN: Wabash College, 1949), xi, and in Arthur W. Shumaker, *A History of Indiana Literature, with Emphasis on the Authors of Imaginative Works Who Commenced Writing Prior to World War II* (Indianapolis: Indiana Historical Society, 1962), 6–7. The raw data came from Alice Payne Hackett, *Fifty Years of Best Sellers, 1895–1945* (New York: R. R. Bowker Company, 1945).

3. Nicholson, "Confessions of a Best-Seller," 207–08.

4. Meredith Nicholson to Henry W. Beers, March 13, 1906, and August 6, 1915, Meredith Nicholson Collection, Manuscript Division, Indiana State Library, Indianapolis; *Indianapolis News*, December 10, 1910.

5. Nicholson, *Provincial American and Other Papers*. Seven of the eight essays first appeared in the *Atlantic Monthly* between 1902 and 1912; the eighth, under a different title, was first in *The Reader* (May 1906). The "Smith" essay attracted considerable attention, prompting countless letters to the editor, sermons, and even a book. Nicholson generously contributed the introduction to the book, *Smith and the Church* (New York, 1913), by the Reverend Henry Harvey Beattys.

6. Nicholson, "Confessions of a Best-Seller," 220–21.

7. Meredith Nicholson to Mr. Wicks, October 23, 1909, Correspondence Files, Indianapolis–Marion County Public Library.

8. Meredith Nicholson, "What I Tried to Do in My Latest Book," *World's Work* 19 (January 1910), 12433–34; see also *Indianapolis News*, December 23, 1909.

9. Nicholson, "What I Tried to Do in My Latest Book."

10. Ibid.

11. Meredith Nicholson to Roger L. Scaife, October 24, 1914, and October 16, 1915, Houghton Mifflin Company Papers, Houghton Library, Harvard University, Cambridge, Massachusetts.

12. Agreement between Meredith Nicholson and Houghton Mifflin Company, June 23, 1910, Meredith Nicholson Contract File, Houghton Mifflin Company Papers.

13. Agreement between Houghton Miffflin Company and American Press Association, October 19, 1910, Houghton Library.

14. See the *Book Review Digest* (1910): 290, for a brief description of the book and excerpts from five reviews.

15. Meredith Nicholson, *The Siege of the Seven Suitors* (Boston: Houghton Mifflin Company, 1910), [v]. Watson (1864–1948), known as "Sunny Jim," was elected in November 1916 to fill the vacancy created by Shively's death. This term ended in 1921, and Watson was elected to full terms in 1920 and 1926.

16. Charles M. Thomas, *Thomas Riley Marshall, Hoosier Statesman* (Oxford, OH: The Mississippi Valley Press, 1939), 62–63. See also James Philip Fadely, *Thomas Taggart: Public Servant, Political Boss, 1856–1929* (Indianapolis: Indiana Historical Society, 1997), for full information on Taggart's career.

17. Meredith Nicholson, "A Postscript by the Chronicler," *A Hoosier Chronicle* (Boston: Houghton Mifflin Company, 1912), 602–[06], the quotations are at 602, 605–6.

18. Maxwell Perkins to Nicholson, December 8, 1920, as quoted in Allegra Stewart, "Meredith Nicholson Revisited" (1988), Allegra Stewart Papers, Special Collections, Rare Books, and University Archives, Irwin Library, Butler University, Indianapolis, 132, 153. Perkins served as one of Nicholson's Scribner editors, particularly on the influential *Valley of Democracy* articles and book in 1918, and later became famous as the editor for both F. Scott Fitzgerald and Thomas Wolfe. For an intriguing account of the influential editor, see A. Scott Berg, *Max Perkins: Editor of Genius* (New York: Pocket Books, 1979 [c. 1978]).

19. Inscription on the copy held by the Indianapolis–Marion County Public Library, as quoted by Stewart, "Nicholson Revisited," 134. Nicholson had other personal favorites too—one being a fictionalized biography, *The Cavalier of Tennessee* (1928), that focused on the early life of Andrew Jackson, and another being his only "history," *The Hoosiers* (1900).

20. *Indianapolis News*, April 12, 1911; Thomas, *Thomas Riley Marshall*, 108, 132.

21. Meredith Nicholson to Robert Underwood Johnson, May 2, 19[1]3?, Johnson Papers, American Academy and Institute of Arts

and Letters, New York. This letter was dated by Nicholson as May 2, 1903, an obvious mistake. For additional information on Lamb, also a close friend of Claude G. Bowers, see Peter J. Sehlinger and Holman Hamilton, *Spokesman for Democracy: Claude G. Bowers, 1878–1958* (Indianapolis: Indiana Historical Society, 2000), 51–52, et passim.

22. A view of this photograph may be seen in Fadely, *Thomas Taggart*, 114, and in Hilton U. Brown, *A Book of Memories* (Indianapolis: Butler University, 1951). In the latter book, the photograph is a double-page spread between pages 200 and 201 and accompanies Brown's chapter, "The Fairbanks Luncheon and Its Participants," 197–204.

23. Nancy Johnson, librarian of the American Academy and Institute of Arts and Letters, to author, October 15, 1985. There is an extended correspondence between Nicholson and Underwood preserved in the Academy files, and the author is grateful to Ms. Johnson for photocopies of these letters

24. *Indianapolis News*, December 29, 1911.

25. "Artist Preserves Mood of Novelist," *Indianapolis Sunday Star*, March 3, 1912. This article appeared alongside two photographs, one of the completed portrait, the other showing the artist at work. The reporter called the new painting "splendid in its coloring as well as in the drawing."

26. *Indianapolis Star*, March 12, 1912. The sailing date from New York was March 23, ship name not known, but the group returned home, probably in May, on the later famous and ill-fated *Lusitania*. Cities on the itinerary included, according to the press report, Paris and Rome, but Nicholson later wrote of having twice visited England, and there is a letter in Virginia that Nicholson wrote from Berlin, so the "Indianapolis caballeros" (McCulloch's term) made an extensive if whirlwind tour of western Europe. See Meredtih Nicholson to Walter P. Eaton, May 5, 1912, Walter P. Eaton Collection, Clifton Waller Barrett Library of American Literature, Special Collections, University of Virginia Library, Charlottesville, and Carleton B. McCulloch to Meredith Nicholson, October 23, 1933, Carleton B. McCulloch Papers, William Henry Smith Memorial Library, Indiana Historical Society, Indianapolis.

27. "Nicholson Named United States Envoy to Lisbon," *Indianapolis Star*, June 19, 1913.

28. Claude G. Bowers to [Frank] Brubeck, June 20, 1913, Claude G. Bowers Papers, Lilly Library, Indiana University, Bloomington.

29. "Nicholson Says He Must Consult Wife before Starting for Portugal," *Indianapolis Star*, June 19, 1913.

30. "Nicholson Will Not Accept the Post of United States Minister," *Indianapolis Star*, June 24, 1913.

31. "Nicholson's Statement," *Indianapolis News*, June 24, 1913.

32. Meredith Nicholson to Ferris Greenslet, July 7, 1916, Houghton Mifflin Company Papers.

33. Robert Cortes Holliday, *Broome Street Straws* (New York: George H. Doran Company, 1919), 184. Holliday devoted an entire chapter of this book to Nicholson, about whom he had also written "at some length" for a New York newspaper. Ibid., 183–86.

34. Ibid. 188–89. Nicholson assured his visitor during a second meeting, after reading his views from the first one, that his calm appearance was just a front, that he was really nervous and excitable at times. Indeed, on his return in 1920, Holliday found a somewhat different Nicholson—busy and a bit imperious for he was caught up in the midst of a political campaign, but he was still friendly and open, and insisted this time that Holliday meet McCulloch, then running for governor and "distinguished" for many other things too. McCulloch was "the physician to the *literati* of Indiana," including Nicholson and Tarkington, and had served in France during the late war as a lieutenant colonel in charge of a military hospital and had received the Croix de Guerre. Holliday considered him distinguished, too, for his wit and charm. Concerning Nicholson, he told how the writer salted his conversation with quotations "in a breath" from Newman, Matthew Arnold, and Ralph Waldo Emerson, and about his habit, when signing the bill at his club, of adding quotations from poets for the waiters' amusement and edification. Holliday also visited the Nicholson home in 1920, and the first thing he saw inside was an extraordinary collection of musical instruments and drums. In another room were a portrait of Tarkington and framed photographs of Henry James and a Union army officer he presumed to be Nicholson's father. After dinner Holliday discovered the musical layout belonged to Tookie, the younger son, whom Holliday identified as the "locally celebrated trap-drummer" who gave a "very fin-

ished performance . . . leaping from place to place, pounding with a
variety of sticks on this and that, in effect all at once." Robert Cortes
Holliday, *Men and Books and Cities* (New York: George H. Doran
Company, 1920), 34–35, 40, 49, 53, 55–56. This book, incidentally,
was dedicated to Nicholson.

35. Meredith Nicholson to Max Farrand, January 16, 1910, and
October 16, 1910, Max Farrand Collection, Huntington Library, San
Marino, California.

36. This booklet was published by the Bobbs-Merrill Company
for the Indiana Society of Chicago, one of the groups to whom it was
presented. Nicholson also read it before a Yale University audience, but
the essay had originated as a presentation for the Indianapolis Literary
Club.

37. *Indianapolis Star*, July 7, 1915; for Nicholson's comment
about his mother, see Stewart, "Meredith Nicholson Revisited," 47.
Sadly, too, just four years later, Margaret Nicholson Noble, the author's
only sibling, also died.

38. For the history of the Riley Memorial Association and valuable biographical sketches of its board members, a veritable who's-
who of central Indiana in the early twentieth century, see Elizabeth
Van Allen and Omer H. Faust, eds., *Keeping the Dream, 1921–1996:
Commemorating 75 Years of Caring for Indiana's Children—James
Whitcomb Riley Memorial Association* (Indianapolis: James Whit-
comb Riley Memorial Association, 1996). On missing Riley, Nicholson
wrote to Ferris Greenslet, July 28, 1916 (Houghton Mifflin Company
Papers); to Senator John W. Kern, June 24, 1916 (Bowers Papers); and
Robert Underwood Johnson, July 27, 1916 (Johnson Papers, National
Academy and Institutes of Arts and Letters, New York).

39. For more information on the "Guard," see George H. Denny,
"Lawton Guard Training Taught Respect for the U.S.," *Indianapolis
Star*, May 22, 1966. The article credited Nicholson with starting the
group for which his son was able to recruit about fifty members.

40. Nicholson's "typewriter" remark is in his author's questionnaire, n. d., Bobbs-Merrill Company Papers, Lilly Library, Indiana University. Other evidence of Nicholson's strong anti-German attitudes are
in portions of the essay, "The Spirit of the West," the concluding chapter of *The Valley of Democracy* (New York: Charles Scribner's Sons,

1918), 235–84. This essay was the subject of an article, "Local Author Shows German Influence Here," *Indianapolis Star*, June 2, 1918. The article also mentioned Nicholson's leadership role in the Vigilantes, an organization of authors, and his efforts to "enlighten readers on situations befogged by German propaganda."

41. *Indianapolis Star*, April 1, 1917.

42. Meredith Nicholson to Roger L. Scaife, April 11, 1917, and October 21, 1917, Houghton Mifflin Company Papers.

43. Ibid., November 3, 1917.

44. See Randolph Bourne, *The History of a Literary Radical and Other Papers by Randolph Bourne* (New York: S. A. Russell, 1956), 285–93, quotation at 288–89.

45. Meredith Nicholson, *Lady Larkspur* (New York: Charles Scribner's Sons, 1919). Another one of Nicholson's light tales, populated with interesting characters faced with unusual choices, and told against the backdrop of a world war, the book received good but not glowing reviews.

Chapter 8

1. Meredith Nicholson, *The Madness of May* (New York: Charles Scribner's Sons, 1917), 34.

2. Hubbard, the creator of the classic comic figure, Abe Martin of Brown County, Indiana, worked at the *Indianapolis News* from 1891 to 1894, while Nicholson was also employed there, and then again from 1901 until his death of a heart attack on December 26, 1930.

3. Nicholson liked to tease McCulloch about the results of that election, in which, at least in Marion County, Nicholson outpolled McCulloch by exactly 3,219 votes. Meredith Nicholson to Carleton McCulloch, January 1, 1936, Carleton B. McCulloch Papers, William Henry Smith Memorial Library, Indiana Historical Society, Indianapolis.

4. A brief history of the shake-up in city government in the late 1920s can be in found in Kris E. Daman's biographical sketch of Mayor John L. Duvall in David J. Bodenhamer and Robert G. Barrows, eds., *Encyclopedia of Indianapolis* (Bloomington and Indianapolis: Indiana University Press, 1994), 517. Nicholson's comment is in his letter to David L. Chambers, April 12, 1928, Bobbs-Merrill Company Papers, Lilly Library, Indiana University, Bloomington.

5. *New York Times*, May 2, 1920.

6. See, for example, Meredith Nicholson to David L. Chambers, February 1, 1930, Bobbs-Merrill Company Papers.

7. This essay first appeared in the *Atlantic Monthly* (July 1916): 175–87. The quotations are at 178, 186, and 187.

8. For a summary of these views and others, see *Book Review Digest* (1921): 320.

9. *New York Times*, May 14, 1922. For other reviews, see *Book Review Digest* (1922): 391.

10. Five other writers joined Nicholson in this publication, including Edna Ferber and Irwin S. Cobb. Editor Long envisioned the book as an evening dinner party, with six distinguished writers relaxing over coffee and discussing their work. In describing each one of his "interesting group," he presciently said that Nicholson was "my idea of an ambassador to the Court of St. James." Ray Long, ed., *My Story That I Like Best* (New York: International Magazine Company, 1925), 7. The remaining three contributors were Peter B. Kyne, James Oliver Curwood, and H. C. Witwer.

11. *Book Review Digest* (1922): 391.

12. Ibid.

13. Editor's introduction to the first installment of Meredith Nicholson's "Broken Barriers," *Cosmopolitan* 72 (January 1922): 12. For the comparison of realisms, see Allegra Stewart, "Meredith Nicholson Revisited" (1988), Allegra Stewart Papers, Special Collections, Rare Books, and University Archives, Irwin Library, Butler University, Indianapolis, 246.

14. "Marion County Alimony Book Started Nicholson Novel," *Indianapolis News*, September 18, 1925.

15. *Indianapolis Star*, April 23, 1922; Stewart, "Meredith Nicholson Revisited," 369; author conversation with Meredith Nicholson III, March 3, 2003.

16. Transcript of interview of Roberta West Nicholson by Allegra Stewart and F. Gerald Handfield Jr., November 16, 1983, 29–30. This interview transcript is in the Allegra Stewart Papers. The Manuscript Division of the Indiana State Library, Indianapolis, has the transcripts of two earlier interviews conducted by Handfield in March 1977, who passed along to me the "from under a rock" comment, not included in the transcripts.

17. Ibid.

18. Ruth Watson to Meredith Nicholson, August 16, 1932, Meredith Nicholson Papers, William Henry Smith Memorial Library, Indiana Historical Society, Indianapolis; Marie Watson to Meredith Nicholson, November 29, 1932, ibid.

19. The publishers were also pleased with the book and promoted it heavily. The Bobbs-Merrill staff even prevailed upon Nicholson, despite the press of duties upon him elsewhere in the summer of 1928, to join in their advertising campaign by attending the National Booksellers Convention in Atlantic City, New Jersey, where the company also distributed hickory canes in honor of Jackson's reputation as "Old Hickory." See David L. Chambers to Meredith Nicholson, April 6, 1928, Bobbs-Merrill Company Papers.

20. Meredith Nicholson, "Shootin' 'em and Stoppin' 'em," *Indianapolis News*, March 16, 1929.

21. Honorary degree files, Meredith Nicholson, 1928, Indiana University Archives, Bloomington. The author thanks university archivist Philip Bantin for supplying me with this item.

22. Meredith Nicholson to Margaret Scott, November 6, 1927, Indiana History Papers, Lilly Library.

23. Meredith Nicholson III Papers, Casa Grande, Arizona. Nicholson proudly showed the author the copy of the book, a birthday present to his father from Riley, with its memorable inscription.

24. One of Nicholson's laudatory comments on Hendricks is in *The Provincial American and Other Papers* (Boston: Houghton Mifflin Company, 1912), 15–16.

25. Many sources are available on the so-called System of 1896 and on Wilson's victory over Taft, abetted by Theodore Roosevelt's leadership of the Bull Moose insurgency in 1912. For an overview of the history of the majority party at that time, see George H. Mayer, *The Republican Party, 1854–1966* (New York: Oxford University Press, 1967); the leading authority on Wilson remains his biographer, Arthur S. Link, who also wrote *Wilson and the Progressive Era, 1910–1917* (New York: Harper and Row, 1954), a volume for the New American Nation series.

26. For an example of the Klan's power and its low-level approach to politics, see the campaign of Democrat William E. Wilson, the

incumbent congressman from Evansville, and how the Klan defeated him. The congressman's son, also William E. Wilson, has brilliantly captured the emotion and fear associated with Indiana politics in 1924 in his account of this dramatic episode, published in the *American Heritage* magazine under the title "Long, Hot Summer in Indiana." This article, originally published in the August 1965 issue of *American Heritage*, has been reprinted in Ralph D. Gray, ed., *Indiana History: A Book of Readings* (Bloomington: Indiana University Press, 1994), 292–302.

27. M. William Luthholtz, *Grand Dragon: D. C. Stephenson and the Ku Klux Klan in Indiana* (West Lafayette: Purdue University Press, 1991), 303–4, 307.

28. Meredith Nicholson, "Hoosier Letters and the Ku Klux," *The Bookman* (March 1928): 7–11.

29. "Nicholson Home Sold to Carl A. Taylor," *Indianapolis News*, November 8, 1920; Meredith Nicholson to Roger Scaife, April 12, 1921, Houghton Mifflin Company Papers, Houghton Library, Harvard University, Cambridge, Massachusetts. The "cliff-dwelling" was the Winter Apartments, located near Meridian and Twelfth streets in downtown Indianapolis.

30. Meredith Nicholson Jr., "5 Year Line-a-Day Diary," November 24, 1916, Meredith Nicholson III Papers.

31. Ibid. This collection of papers includes, in addition to young Nicholson's five-year diary, the very interesting yearbooks from Milford School for 1921 and 1922.

32. Roberta West Nicholson interview, November 16, 1983; see also Elizabeth's obituary in the *Indianapolis Star*, September 13, 1951.

33. Roberta West Nicholson interview, November 16, 1983.

34. Charles L. Nicholson lived on North Delaware Street, and his office was in the Circle Tower Building downtown. A nervous breakdown led to his early death in 1949. *Indianapolis Star*, March 23, 1949.

35. Roberta West Nicholson interview, November 16, 1983, passim.

36. This information on the West family has come from Meredith Nicholson III Papers and his recollections. Typhoon once the held the track record at Dade Park near Evansville but finished fifteenth of eighteen in the 1928 Derby. Conversation with Meredith Nicholson III, March 26, 2005.

37. Ibid.; Roberta West Nicholson interview.
38. *Indianapolis Star*, December 22, 1931.

Chapter 9

1. Meredith Nicholson, "The Land of the Tall Poinsettia," *American Foreign Service Journal* 11 (October 1934): 517.

2. See H. H. Howland, "The University Club of Indianapolis," *The Bookman* 22 (January 1906), 463–68. Both McCulloch and Stout were prominent men in the city. McCulloch served as the medical director of the State Life Insurance Company, the same company that Meredith Nicholson Jr. joined in 1945 and eventually headed. Stout, a graduate of Earlham College and Harvard Law School, was one of the leading bankers in the city. He also chaired the executive committee of the Indianapolis Power and Light Company, which honored him in 1958 by dedicating its $133,000,000 generating station on South Harding Street in his name. On McCulloch, see Elizabeth Van Allen and Omer H. Foust, eds., *Keeping the Dream, 1921–1996: Commemorating 75 Years of Caring for Indiana's Children—James Whitcomb Riley Memorial Association* (Indianapolis: James Whitcomb Riley Memorial Association, 1996), 116–17; on Stout, see the *Indianapolis Star*, May 7, 1962.

3. Franklin Delano Roosevelt, *The New Leadership* (1932). The author is indebted to Allegra Stewart for this reference and to the archivist of the Roosevelt Presidential Library in Hyde Park for copies of the exchange of notes in 1932: Nicholson to Roosevelt, November 9, 1932; Roosevelt to Nicholson, December 5, 1932.

4. The appointment details are contained in Nicholson's "123" or personnel file, Record Group 59, U.S. National Archives and Records Administration, Washington, D.C. (hereafter cited as NARA). See especially the initial cable from Hull to Nicholson, August 11, 1933, his reply of August 12, 1933, and the letter from Acting Secretary of State Wilbur Lane to Nicholson, August 24, 1933, spelling out some details of the appointment. Nicholson was sworn in shortly before his departure from Indianapolis. Friend and political ally Mayor Reginald H. Sullivan administered the oath of office in a brief city hall ceremony that was broadcast on local radio. *Indianapolis Star*, September 7, 1933.

5. Minutes of Committee, Dinner in Honor of Meredith Nicholson, August 22, 1933, Bobbs-Merrill Company Papers, Lilly Library, Indiana University, Bloomington.

6. Carleton B. McCulloch, "A Tribute of an Old Friend," *Indianapolis Star*, September 3, 1933.

7. Everett C. Watkins, "Nicholson May Serve as Peacemaker in Romantic and Primitive Paraguay," *Indianapolis Star*, August 20, 1933. See also the *Indianapolis News*, August 19, 1933.

8. *Indianapolis News*, September 18, 1933; *Indianapolis Star*, September 19, 1933.

9. Meredith Nicholson to Dorothy Lannon, October 9, 1933, Meredith Nicholson Papers, William Henry Smith Memorial Library, Indiana Historical Society, Indianapolis.

10. Meredith Nicholson to Carleton B. McCulloch, September 29, 1933, Carleton B. McCulloch Papers, William Henry Smith Memorial Library, Indiana Historical Society, Indianapolis.

11. Ibid.

12. Meredith Nicholson to Carleton B. McCulloch, November 10, 1933, McCulloch Papers. The details about travel arrangements come from a cable to the Department of State, September 30, 1933, in Nicholson's "123" File, RG 59, NARA.

13. Meredith Nicholson to Carleton B. McCulloch, November 10 1933, McCulloch Papers.

14. Ibid.

15. Ibid.

16. Nicholson's "123" File, Documents 19 and 23, RG 59, NARA.

17. *Indianapolis Star*, March 11, 1934.

18. Hubert C. Herring, *A History of Latin American from the Beginnings to the Present* (New York: Alfred A. Knopf, 1955), 678, and Riordan Roelt and Richard Scott Sachs, *Paraguay: The Personalist Legacy* (Boulder, CO: Westview Press, 1991), passim. For an overview of the Chaco War, see *The Chaco Peace Conference: Report of the Delegation of the United States of America to the Peace Conference Held at Buenos Aires July 1, 1935–January 23, 1939* (Washington, DC: Government Printing Office, 1940).

19. Roelt and Sachs, *Paraguay*, x.

270

20. Meredith Nicholson, "General Conditions Prevailing in Paraguay for the Period October 1, 1933, to October 31, 1933," State Department Records, Latin America, RG 59, NARA.

21. Ibid. The January 15, 1934, report covered the period from November 1, 1933, to December 31, 1933.

22. Ibid.

23. Ibid., in the reports for April and June 1934.

24. Nicholson, "Land of the Tall Poinsettia," 519, 554.

25. Nicholson, "General Conditions Prevailing in Paraguay," November 1933, State Department Records, Latin America, RG 59, NARA.

26. Carleton B. McCulloch to Meredith Nicholson, September 11, 1933, Meredith Nicholson to Carleton B. McCulloch, October 13, 1933, McCulloch Papers.

27. McCulloch to Nicholson, April, 21, August 2, September 4, and October 15, 1934, ibid.

28. McCulloch to Nicholson, addendum, dated February 7, to letter of January 26, 1934; McCulloch to Nicholson, December 14, 1933, ibid.

29. McCulloch to Nicholson, March 1, 1934, and February 7, 1935, ibid.

30. McCulloch to Nicholson, February 7, 1935, ibid.

31. Nicholson to McCulloch, April 4 and October 13, 1934, ibid.

32. Nicholson to McCulloch, April 4, 1934, ibid.

33. Nicholson to McCulloch, January 12, 1935, ibid.; Meredith Nicholson to David L. Chambers, January 30, 1935, Bobbs-Merrill Papers., Lilly Library, Indiana University.

34. Nicholson to McCulloch, December 12, 1934, McCulloch Papers.

35. McCulloch to Nicholson, January 11, 1935, ibid.

Chapter 10

1. Meredith Nicholson, *Broken Barriers* (New York: Charles Scribner's Sons, 1922), 69.

2. Mary Lou Weddle to Dorothy Nicholson, February 3, 1935, Meredith Nicholson Papers, William Henry Smith Memorial Library, Indiana Historical Society, Indianapolis.

3. "Mansion to Be Occupied by Nicholson," *Indianapolis Star*, January 8, 1935.

4. John Gunther, *Inside Latin America* (New York: Harper, 1941), 178, 182–83; Hubert C. Herring, *A History of Latin America from the Beginnings to the Present* (New York: Alfred A. Knopf, 1955), 468.

5. Carleton B. McCulloch to Meredith Nicholson, May 9 and July 31, 1935; Meredith Nicholson to Carleton B. McCulloch, July 20 and December 3, 1935, Carleton B. McCulloch Papers, William Henry Smith Memorial Library, Indiana Historical Society, Indianapolis.

6. Roberta West Nicholson interview, November 16, 1983, Allegra Stewart Papers, Special Collections, Rare Books, and University Archives, Irwin Library, Butler University, Indianapolis.

7. Meredith Nicholson to Dorothy Nicholson, March 23, 1940, Meredith Nicholson Papers.

8. Meredith Nicholson to Carleton B. McCulloch, January 28, 1936, McCulloch Papers.

9. Meredith Nicholson to Claude G. Bowers, February 11, 1936, Claude Bowers Ppaers, Lilly Library, Indiana University, Bloomington; Nicholson to McCulloch, January 7, 1936, McCulloch Papers.

10. Nicholson called his article, "Hoosier Reminisces in Far-Off Caracas," but it was printed under the headline "Nicholson Recalls Former Faces and Figures," with his own title as the subhead, in the *Indianapolis News*, February 5, 1936; McCulloch to Nicholson, February 10, 1936, McCulloch Papers; Meredith Nicholson to Margaret Shipp, March 22, 1936, Meredith Nicholson Papers.

11. Nicholson to McCulloch, January 7, 1936, McCulloch Papers.

12. Meredith Nicholson to David L. Chambers, March 3, 1936, Bobbs-Merrill Papers, Lilly Library, Indiana University; *Indianapolis Star*, December 5, 1936.

13. Nicholson to McCulloch, February 3, 1936, McCulloch Papers; Meredith Nicholson's "123" file, State Department, RG 59, U.S. National Archives and Records Administration, Washington, D.C. (hereafter cited as NARA).

14. Nicholson to McCulloch, November 6, 1934, McCulloch Papers; "Funerales en Memoria de Mr. Frederick Grabb [*sic*]," Cara-

cas newspaper clipping enclosed in Nicholson to McCulloch, May 10, 1937, ibid.

15. Nicholson to McCulloch, February 3, 1936, ibid.

16. Cordell Hull telegram to Meredith Nicholson, February 23, 1938, Nicholson's "123" file, State Department, RG 59, NARA.

17. In Roberta West Nicholson's three recorded interviews with historians, various bits and pieces of this story came out, but without any details. See the oral history transcripts of these interviews, with F. Gerald Handfield Jr. of the Indiana State Library, on March 11 and March 16, 1977, and with Handfield and Allegra Stewart on November 16, 1983, Manuscripts Division of the Indiana State Library and the Special Collections, Rare Books, and University Archives of the Irwin Library at Butler University, both in Indianapolis. Nicholson told McCulloch, shortly after his transfer, that he regretted not being able to give him the "inside history" of the move, and later said only that the recent "shuffle" of diplomats in Latin America was designed to "put Mr. Farley's friend in Caracas." Nicholson to McCulloch, May 12 and June 15, 1938, McCulloch Papers.

18. Nicholson to McCulloch, May 23, 1938, McCulloch Papers.

19. Gunther, *Inside Latin America*, 137.

20. Nicholson to McCulloch, April 15 and August 19, 1938, McCulloch Papers.

21. Gabry Rivas, "If There Existed an Order of Rubén Darío," *La Nueva Prenza*, as translated and published in the *Indianapolis Star*, March 4, 1941.

22. Nicholson to McCulloch, August 12 and September 26, 1939, McCulloch Papers.

23. "Nicaraguan President Will Visit City For Hour, May 21, On Way to Purdue," *Indianapolis Star*, May 10, 1939. Another schedule change, in order for Somoza to "give away" the bride in a wedding at the Nicaraguan Legation in Washington, D.C., delayed his arrival in Indianapolis until May 25. *Indianapolis News*, May 20, 1939.

24. "Warm Hoosier Welcome Given President Somoza in Brief Visit," *Indianapolis News*, May 25, 1939.

25. Ibid.

26. "Somoza Draws 'First Milk' in Best Hoosier Manner," *Indianapolis Star*, May 26, 1939.

27. Meredith Nicholson to David L. Chambers, October 28, 1937, Bobbs-Merrill Papers.

28. Ernie Pyle, "Hoosier Vagabond," *Indianapolis Times*, February 24, 1940.

29. Ibid., February 26, 1940.

30. Ibid.

31. Ibid.

32. Meredith Nicholson to Dorothy Nicholson, March 22, 1940, Meredith Nicholson Papers; Nicholson to McCulloch, February 6, 1940, McCulloch Papers. Nicholson reported to his doctor, McCulloch, a weight loss from 180 to 150 pounds while in Managua.

Chapter 11

1. Meredith Nicholson, *Short Flights* (Indianapolis: Bowen-Merrill, 1891), 68.

2. Allegra Stewart, "Meredith Nicholson Revisited" (1988), Allegra Stewart Papers, Special Collections, Rare Books, and University Archives, Irwin Library, Butler University, Indianapolis, 369.

3. Meredith Nicholson to Carleton B. McCulloch, April 22, 1941, Carleton B. McCulloch Papers, William Henry Smith Memorial Library, Indiana Historical Society, Indianapolis.

4. McCulloch to Nicholson, November 27, 1941, ibid.

5. Clipping enclosed in Nicholson to McCulloch, December 19, 1941, ibid.

6. Nicholson to McCulloch, December 13, 1942, ibid.

7. Nicholson to McCulloch, August 16, 1942, ibid.

8. See Jeannette Covert Nolan's "Lines with a Hoosier Accent" column titled "[Birthday] Greetings to an Indiana Celebrity," *Indianapolis Star*, December 8, 1943.

9. *Indianapolis Star*, December 25, 1943.

10. A few letters in the Meredith Nicholson Collection at the Indiana Historical Society reveal Dorothy's activities, the loss of some personal belongings in transit from Florida, and an accounting of her assets in 1944—personal property valued at $450, $140 in cash, and "no husband." Even Dorothy's age is not known, although she must have been slightly younger than Meredith.

11. Queries to the Grant County historian and to the head of the Marion, Indiana, public library have been fruitless. Neither person could provide any information on Dorothy Wolfe Lannon or her family, supposedly from Marion and Grant County. Nor could genealogists at the Fort Wayne Public Library discover anything about her origins or fate.

12. This comment is part of his column on "The Heroic Reporters" that mentioned John Gunther and Ernie Pyle, among many others. *Indianapolis Star*, August 16, 1943. Nicholson's time in the newspaper world may have seemed like fourteen years, but the records indicate that he was so employed for twelve years.

13. Russell Pulliam, *Publisher Gene Pulliam, Last of the Newspaper Titans* (Ottawa, IL: Jameson Books, 1984), 105–7. Although Nicholson and Nolan are not mentioned specifically here, Pulliam did acquire the paper in 1944 with intent to reform it.

14. "Profile of the Week," *Indianapolis Times*, July 26, 1941.

15. Ibid.

16. Ibid.

17. Roberta West Nicholson interview, November 16, 1983, Stewart Papers.

18. *Indianapolis News*, January 18, 1947. The *Indianapolis Times*, December 12, 1947, also carried a late-in-life photograph of Nicholson with his friend and physician McCulloch.

19. *New York Times*, December 22, 1947.

20. Lamb's poem, "The Old Familiar Faces," can be found in a recent biography of his sister, *Mad Mary Lamb: Lunacy and Murder in Literary London*, by Susan Tyler Hitchcock (New York: W. W. Norton, 2005), 87–88. The Matthew Arnold quotation appears, inter alia, in the opening paragraph of Nicholson's last published article, "In Tune with the Times," *Indianapolis Times*, September 27, 1947. The brief words from Walt Whitman were often used by Nicholson in letters to McCulloch during the late 1930s and early 1940s as he deplored the absence of outstanding Indiana congressmen at that time and equated their isolationism ("assolationism") with the Copperheadism of Abraham Lincoln's time.

SELECT BIBLIOGRAPHY

Books by Meredith Nicholson

Short Flights. Indianapolis: Bowen-Merrill, 1891.

The Hoosiers. New York: Macmillan, 1900.

The Main Chance. Indianapolis: Bobbs-Merrill Co., 1903.

Zelda Dameron. Indianapolis: Bobbs-Merrill Co., 1904.

The House of a Thousand Candles. Indianapolis: Bobbs-Merrill Co., 1905.

Poems. Indianapolis: Bobbs-Merrill Co., 1906.

The Port of Missing Men. Indianapolis: Bobbs-Merrill Co., 1907.

Rosalind at Red Gate. Indianapolis: Bobbs-Merrill Co., 1907.

The Little Brown Jug at Kildare. Indianapolis: Bobbs-Merrill Co., 1908.

The Lords of High Decision. New York: Doubleday, Page, and Co., 1909.

The Siege of the Seven Suitors. Boston: Houghton Mifflin Co., 1910.

A Hoosier Chronicle. Boston: Houghton Mifflin Co., 1912.

The Provincial American and Other Papers. Boston: Houghton Mifflin Co., 1912.

Otherwise Phyllis. Boston: Houghton Mifflin Co., 1913.

The Poet. Boston: Houghton Mifflin Co., 1914.

The Proof of the Pudding. Boston: Houghton Mifflin Co., 1916.

The Madness of May. New York: Charles Scribner's Sons, 1917.

A Reversible Santa Claus. Boston: Houghton Mifflin Co., 1917.

The Valley of Democracy. New York: Charles Scribner's Sons, 1918.

Lady Larkspur. New York: Charles Scribner's Sons, 1919.

Blacksheep! Blacksheep! New York: C. Scribner's Sons, 1920.

The Man in the Street: Papers on American Topics. New York: C. Scribner's Sons, 1921.

Honor Bright: A Comedy in Three Acts. (a play, with Kenyon Nicholson). New York. 1921.

Best Laid Schemes. New York: Charles Scribner's Sons, 1922.

Broken Barriers. New York: Charles Scribner's Sons, 1922.

The Hope of Happiness. New York: Charles Scribner's Sons, 1923.

And They Lived Happily Ever After! New York: Charles Scribner's
 Sons, 1925.

The Cavalier of Tennessee. Indianapolis: Bobbs-Merrill Co., 1928.

Old Familiar Faces. Indianapolis: Bobbs-Merrill Co., 1929.

Other sources, including major articles by Meredith Nicholson

Banta, R.E. *Indiana Authors and Their Books, 1816–1916: Biographical
 Sketches of Authors Who Published During the first Century of
 Statehood, with Lists of Their Books.* Crawfordsville, IN: Wabash
 College, 1949.

Berg, A. Scott. *Max Perkins: Editor of Genius.* New York: Dutton,
 1978.

Bodenhamer, David J. and Robert G. Barrows, eds., *Encyclopedia of
 Indianapolis.* Bloomington: Indiana University Press, 1994.

Brown, Hilton U. *A Book of Memories.* Indianapolis: Butler
 University, 1951.

*The Chaco Peace Conference: Report of the Delegation of the United
 States of America to the Peace Conference Held at Buenos Aires
 July 1, 1935–January 23, 1939.* Government Printing Office:
 Washington, D.C., 1940.

Dean, Eric T. Jr. *Shook Over Hell: Post-Traumatic Stress, Vietnam, and
 the Civil War.* Cambridge, MA: Harvard University Press, 1997.

Downey, Lawrence J. *A Live Thing in the Whole Town: The History
 of the Indianapolis–Marion County Public Library, 1873–1990.*
 Indianapolis: Indianapolis–Marion County Public Library
 Foundation, 1991.

Fadely, James Philip. *Thomas Taggart: Public Servant, Political Boss.*
 Indianapolis: Indiana Historical Society, 1997.

Geib, George W. *Indianapolis: Hoosiers' Circle City.* Tulsa, OK:
 Continental Heritage Press, 1981.

Gnat, Raymond E., comp., and Lawrence S. Connor, ed., *The
 Indianapolis Literary Club: Summarized Record, 1976–2003;
 To Which Is Appended Historical Reminiscences and Vignettes.*
 Indianapolis: Indianapolis Literary Club Foundation, 2004.

Gray, Ralph D., ed., *The Hoosier State: Readings in Indiana History*. 2 vols. Grand Rapids, MI: William B. Erdmann's Co., 1980.

———. "Indiana Bookshelf: The Centennial of *The Hoosiers*," *Traces of Indiana and Midwestern History*, 12 (Fall 2000), 42–44.

———. "'The Most Rabid of Hoosiers,' Meredith Nicholson," *Traces of Indiana and Midwestern History*, 9 (Spring 1997), 14–21.

Gunther, John. *Inside Latin America*. New York: Harper and Brothers, 1941.

Hackett, Alice Payne. *Fifty Years of Best Sellers, 1895–1945*. New York: R. R. Bowker Co., 1945.

Herring, Hubert. *A History of Latin American from the Beginnings to the Present*. New York: Alfred A. Knopf, 1955,

Holliday, Robert. *Broom Street Straws*. New York: George H. Doran Co., 1919.

———. *Men and Books and Cities*. New York: George H. Doran Co., 1920.

Latham, Charles Jr. *William Fortune (1863–1942): A Hoosier Biography*. Indianapolis: Guild Press of Indiana, 1994.

Leary, Edward A. *Indianapolis: The Story of a City*. Indianapolis: Bobbs-Merrill Co., 1970).

de la Mare, Walter, ed. *Selected Letters of George Edward Woodberry*. Boston: Houghton Mifflin Co., 1933.

McCulloch, Carleton B. "A Tribute [to Nicholson] of an Old Friend," *Indianapolis Star*, September 3, 1933.

Miller, John W. *Indiana Newspaper Bibliography: Historical Accounts of All Indiana Newspapers from 1804 to 1980 and Locational Information for All Available Copies, both Original and Microfilm* (Indianapolis: Indiana Historical Society, 1982).

Nicholson, Meredith. "An Ancient and Honorable Society [The Indianapolis Literary Club]," *Indianapolis Star*, March 2, 1944.

———. "A Brief Story of His Life Told by Himself," *Indianapolis Star*, October 20, 1918

———. "Confessions of a Best-Seller." *Atlantic Monthly* 97 (November 1909). Reprinted in *The Provincial American and Other Papers.* Boston: Houghton Mifflin Co., 1912.

———. "Edward Eggleston." *Atlantic Monthly* 90 (December 1902): 804–9.

———. "A Hoosier Boyhood." *Youth's Companion* (December 9, 1915). Reprinted in Charity Dye, *Some Torch Bearers in Indiana*. Indianapolis: Hollenbeck Press, 1917.

———. "Hoosier Letters and the Ku Klux." *The Bookman* (March 1928): 7–11.

———. "Hoosier Reminisces in Far-Away Caracas." *Indianapolis News*, February 5, 1936.

———. "Indianapolis: A City of Homes." *Atlantic Monthly* 93 (June 1904): 836–45.

———. "James Whitcomb Riley." *Atlantic Monthly* 108 (October 1916): 503–14.

———. "The Land of the Tall Poinsettia." *American Foreign Service Journal* 11 (October 1934): 517–19, 554–55.

———. "Lew Wallace as Meredith Nicholson Knew Him." *Indianapolis Star*, January 9, 1910.

———. "The Second Rate Man in Politics." *Atlantic Monthly* 118 (August 1916): 175–87.

———. "Tale of a Postage Stamp." *Chicago Tribune*, February 20, 1886.

———. "The Third Man." In Ray Long, ed., *My Story That I Liked Best* (New York: International Magazine Co., 1925.

———. "A Virginia Impression: Washington and Lee." *The Phi Gamma Delta* (November 1905): 72–77.

———. "What I Tried to Do in My Latest Book." *World's Work* 19 (January 1910): 12433–34.

———. "Without Benefit of College." In *Old Familiar Faces*. Indianapolis: Bobbs-Merrill Co., 1929. This essay originally appeared in *Good Housekeeping* (January 1926).

Nicholson, Roberta West. Interview, by Allegra Stewart and F. Gerald Handfield Jr. November 16, 1983. A transcript of this interview is in the Allegra Stewart Papers, Special Collections, Rare Books, and University Archives, Irwin Library, Butler University, Indianapolis.

———. Interview, by F. Gerald Handfield Jr. March 11 and March 16, 1977. Transcripts of these conversations are in the Manuscript Section, Indiana Division of the Indiana State Library, Indianapolis.

Phillips, Clifton J. *Indiana in Transition: The Emergence of an Industrial Commonwealth, 1880–1920*. Indianapolis: Indiana Historical Bureau and Indiana Historical Society, 1968.

Roelt, Riordan, and Richard Scott Sachs. *Paraguay: The Personalist Legacy*. Boulder, CO: Westview Press, 1991.

Russo, Dorothy Ritter, and Thelma Lois Sullivan, comps. *Bibliographical Studies of Seven Authors of Crawfordsville, Indiana: Lew and Susan Wallace, Maurice and Will Thompson, Mary Hannah and Caroline Virginia Krout, and Meredith Nicholson*. Indianapolis: Indiana Historical Society, 1952.

Sehlinger, Peter J., and Holman Hamilton. *Spokesman for Democracy: Claude G. Bowers, 1878–1958*. Indianapolis: Indiana Historical Society, 2000.

Shumaker, Arthur W. *A History of Indiana Literature, with Emphasis on the Authors of Imaginative Works Who Commenced Writing Prior to World War II*. Indianapolis: Indiana Historical Bureau, 1962.

Thomas, Charles M. *Thomas Riley Marshall, Hoosier Statesman*. Oxford, OH: The Mississippi Valley Press, 1939.

Thornbrough, Emma Lou. *Indiana in the Civil War Era, 1850–1880*. Indianapolis: Indiana Historical Bureau and Indiana Historical Society, 1965.

Van Allen, Elizabeth, and Omer H. Faust, eds. *Keeping the Dream, 1921–1996: Commemorating 75 Years of Caring for Indiana's Children—James Whitcomb Riley Memorial Association*. Indianapolis: James Whitcomb Riley Memorial Association, 1996.

Woodress, James. *Booth Tarkington: Gentleman from Indiana*. Philadelphia: J. B. Lippincott Co., 1954.